In this the love of God was manifested [shown] toward us, that God has sent His only begotten Son into the world, that we might live through Him. In this is love, not that we loved God, but that He loved us and sent His Son to be the propitiation [atoning sacrifice] for our sins.

—1 John 4:9–10

We love Him because He first loved us.

—1 John 4:19

Michael Christian

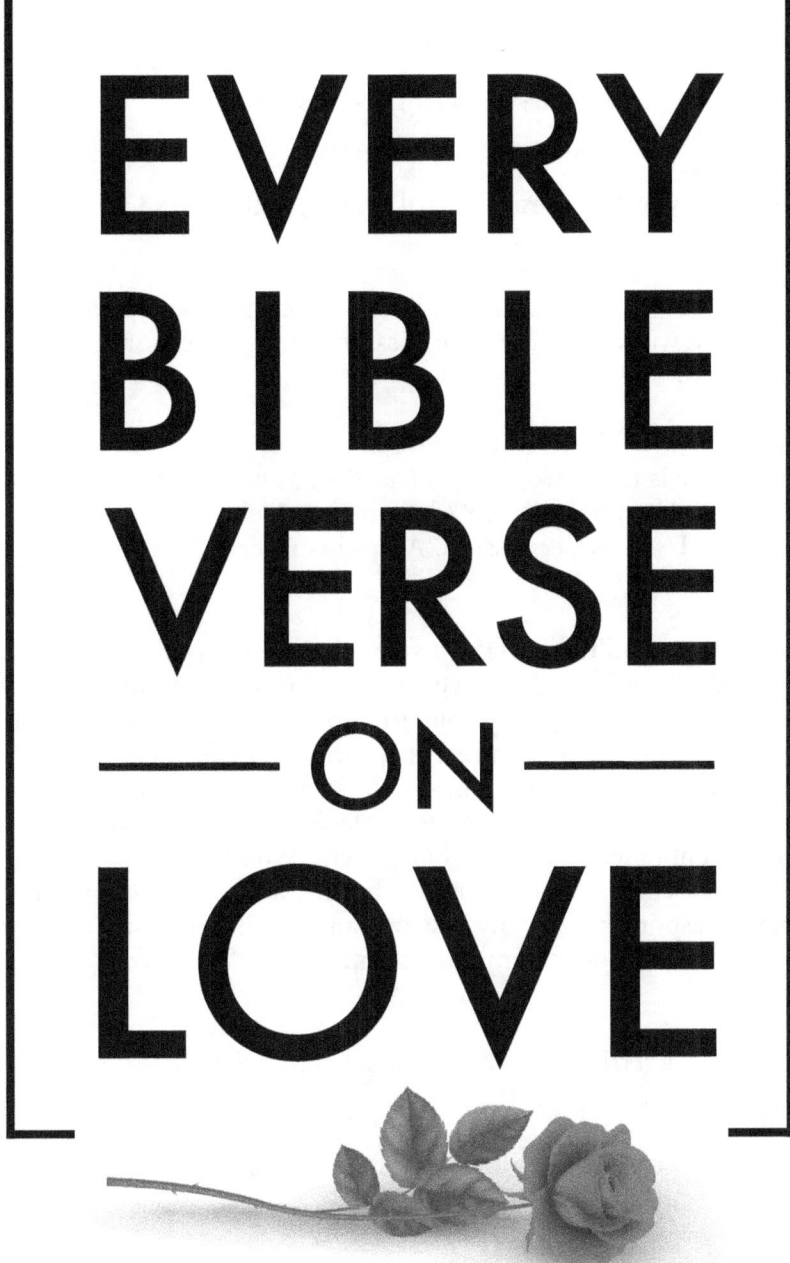

EVERY BIBLE VERSE ON LOVE

The Bible Course on Love with
Greek and Hebrew Definitions

TWIN PILLARS PRESS

PARADISE • CALIFORNIA

© 2024 Michael D. Christian

ISBN 978-0-9894610-4-7

Library of Congress Control Number: 2024908338

All rights reserved. No portion of this book or cover may be reproduced in any form without written permission from the author.

Unless otherwise indicated,
Scripture is taken from *The New King James Version®*.
Copyright © 1982 by Thomas Nelson.
Used by permission. All rights reserved.

The author loves Jesus and the Bible and strongly believes that following Biblical teachings is eternally beneficial. However, in offering spiritual advice, neither the author nor the publisher is engaged in rendering professional counseling or services to the reader. The author does not present spiritual guidelines as a substitute for medical care or licensed clergy or clinical counseling. This book's ideas, suggestions, and procedures are not intended to replace professional guidance. Those with physical or mental health concerns are advised to see an appropriate doctor or a licensed clergy or clinical counselor. Neither the author nor the publisher shall be held liable or responsible for any loss or damage allegedly arising from any suggestion or information contained in this book.

Cover/Interior Design: Michael Christian

Published by Twin Pillars Press
P. O. Box 531
Paradise, CA 95967

Find more Bible study resources at *https://michaelchristian.us*.
For quantity pricing, please contact *CustomerService@michaelchristian.us*.

Printed in the United States of America.

Table of Contents

INTRODUCTORY ARTICLES

- How This Book "Happened" 7
- Getting the Most from This Book 10
- Experiencing God's Love for the First Time .. 13
- Is Love Growing Cold? 17
- It's All About the Word 19
- Why a Topical Word Study? 22
- Scripture Handwriting and Engaging Your Brain .. 24
- Renewing Your Mind Requires Prayer 30
- Hurt? Wounded? Discouraged? Feel Like God Let You Down? 33

PART I: THE WORD LOVE THROUGHOUT THE NEW TESTAMENT

NEW TESTAMENT GREEK WORD SECTIONS

- Word 1. Agapao 47
- Word 2. Agape 60
- The "Love Chapter" 67
- Word 3. Agapetos 72
- Word 4. Astorgos 74
- Word 5. Philadelphia 75
- Word 6. Philadelphos 76
- Word 7. Philagathos 77
- Word 8. Philandros 78
- Word 9. Philanthropia 79
- Word 10. Philarguria 80
- Word 11. Philarguros 82
- Word 12. Philautos 83
- Word 13. Philedonos 84
- Word 14. Phileo 85
- Word 15. Philoproteuo 87
- Word 16. Philoteknos 89
- Word 17. Philotheos 90
- Word 18. Prosphiles 92
- Word 19. Thelo 94

NEW TESTAMENT VERSE CONCORDANCE. 99

PART II: THE WORD LOVE THROUGHOUT THE OLD TESTAMENT

OLD TESTAMENT HEBREW WORD SECTIONS

    Word 1. 'Agab 123
    Word 2. 'Agabim. 124
    Word 3. 'Ahab 125
    Word 4. 'Ahabah 128
    Word 5. 'Ahabim. 129
    Word 6. Dod 130
    Word 7. 'Etnan 131
    Word 8. Habab 132
    Word 9. Hamudot 133
    Word 10. Hashaq 134
    Word 11. Hesed 135
    Word 12. Mahmad 138
    Word 13. Na'ah 139
    Word 14. Na'veh 141
    Word 15. 'Ohabim. 142
    Word 16. Raham 143
    Word 17. Ra'yah 145
    Word 18. Rea' 146
    Word 19. Sane' 148
    Word 20. Shappir 149
    Word 21. Tob 150
    Word 22. Yadid 153
    Word 23. Yapheh 154
    Word 24. Yedidut 155

OLD TESTAMENT VERSE CONCORDANCE 159

PRAYER 189

SELF-STUDY QUESTIONS. 190

BIBLIOGRAPHY 192

INTRODUCTORY ARTICLES

But God, who is rich in mercy, because of His great love with which He loved us, even when we were dead in trespasses, made us alive together with Christ (by grace you have been saved), and raised us up together, and made us sit together in the heavenly places in Christ Jesus, that in the ages to come He might show the exceeding riches of His grace in His kindness toward us in Christ Jesus.

—Ephesians 2:4–7

Therefore be imitators of God as dear children.
And walk in love, as Christ also has loved us
And given Himself for us,
An offering and a sacrifice to God
For a sweet-smelling aroma.

—Ephesians 5:1–2

HOW THIS BOOK "HAPPENED"

I didn't know that going to work that day would lead to a brush with death. I was 23, a newly born-again Christian doing temporary work on an oil drilling rig. That night, a thick steel pin broke in the lifting mechanism high above me. It caused pieces of heavy steel to crash to the drilling floor where I was repairing a cable.

A minute earlier, something impressed me to move a little to the right. I did, and God's impression saved my life.

For in the next instant, a piece of falling metal hit the back of my hard hat and knocked me unconscious. It grazed and fractured my shoulder blade, leaving a six-inch crater in the steel deck plate before ricocheting sixty feet into the night. I was a fraction of an inch from not being here today.

One of the crew took me to the hospital. They x-rayed my shoulder, saw the fracture, cleaned a small wound on my back, and sent me home. My shoulder healed quickly, but my brain had suffered a serious concussion. It would take more time.

When I prayed for wisdom about my healing process, the Holy Spirit impressed me to hand copy Scriptures four hours a day. He led me to copy every verse in the New Testament that contained the word *love*.

What I knew about love wouldn't have filled a small measuring cup. I loved my dog, I loved ice cream, and I was learning to love my wife. To me, love was the emotion I felt when someone made *me* feel good. I was shocked to discover the second New Testament verse on love said, *"Love your enemies."* (Matt. 5:43–44) I had no idea how anyone could do that.

Writing out God's verses on love began my education on the most challenging subject in the Bible. The Lord not only instructs us to love our enemies, but Him, our spouse, family, fellow Christians, and neighbors. Walking in love demands the highest level of spiritual maturity, and I stood on the lowest rung of that ladder.

Hand copying verses became life-changing. As I focused on God's Word, I began to understand the God of the Bible. He quit being a "concept" and became a real Person. Hand copying Scripture is perhaps the best method of meditating in the Bible. I describe how this works in detail on page 24, "Scripture Handwriting and Engaging Your Brain."

God's College Level Course on Love

Because God's Word is inspired, the *verse lists* on the subject of love are inspired. They contain what God wants us to know about love. These verses introduced me to what could be called *God's college level course on love*. I doubt any college or seminary offers it. But it's a very practical course, and you can take it the same way I did, by studying this book.

As I wrote out the Scriptures, I learned about the highest kind of love, the *agape* love of God. Jesus demonstrated it so beautifully by sacrificing Himself for us on the cross. He commanded us to love others as He loved us. What a self-sacrificing love He modeled!

But there is more to the subject of love than *agape,* as important as it is. The Bible speaks of various forms of human love, including the love of friendship and family. It commends women who love their husbands and children. It exhorts men to love their wives and families as Christ loves the church.

God's course on love warns against being a lover of self, a lover of money, or a lover of pleasure more than a lover of God.

Pastors and overseers need to be "a lover of what is good." Anyone can see the bad in people, but the pastoral gift uncovers and encourages the good in everyone.

One elder in a New Testament congregation "loved" the power of his position so much that in his pride he opposed the apostle John and had to be replaced.

These and the other lessons in this book have shaped my life. I am not perfect, but I am so much further ahead in my love walk because I made time to hand copy God's verses on love.

My brain healed quickly as I wrote out Scripture, for the Lord is our healer. But I was learning so much that I didn't want to quit after I was better. I chose another word to copy, then another, and another. I continued this practice for over twenty years, sometimes writing out whole books of the Bible.

I once estimated that I had spent at least 10,000 hours hand writing God's Word. But the reward is not in patting oneself on the back but in getting to know the Author.

Thus says the Lord:

> "Let not the wise man glory in his wisdom,
> Let not the mighty man glory in his might,
> Nor let the rich man glory in his riches;
> But let him who glories glory in this,
> *That he understands and knows Me,*
> That I am the Lord, exercising lovingkindness, judgment, and righteousness in the earth.
> For in these I delight," says the LORD. —Jeremiah 9:23–24 (italics added)

When you make the commitment to meditate in God's Word, the Holy Spirit sees your heart and comes to tutor you. (John 16:13, 1 John 2:27, John 14:26) He is the best Teacher because He helps you *understand* what you are reading. Plus, He whispers practical words of daily guidance between the lines, if you know what I mean.

I appeal to you to set aside time to read God's inspired course on love, digest its meaning, copy the Scriptures, and allow the Holy Spirit to mold and shape your life. As you do, the *personal contact* you'll have with the Lord will be beyond anything you've known. Jesus issued you an invitation, "Come to Me." (Matt. 11:28, Rev. 22:17) James wrote, "Draw near to God, and He will draw near to you." (James 4:8)

Will you respond to His invitation? If so, you can simply pray, "Come, Holy Spirit. Teach me to love like Jesus loves. Fill me with the wisdom of Your Word. Help me apply the Word to my life and relationships. In Jesus' name. Amen." The Lord loves and instructs those whose hearts turn toward Him. Pray into the wisdom of God's Word on love today. Your life will never be the same!

GETTING THE MOST FROM THIS BOOK

Love is central to the Bible, and *Every Bible Verse on Love* walks you through love's meanings from Genesis to Revelation. English has one main word for love. But the Bible's original Greek and Hebrew have many words, each with its own nuance of meaning. This book assists you in understanding the varied facets of love so you may apply their lessons to your life.

The book has three divisions.

- Introductory Articles lay a foundation for studying and meditating in the Word. One article introduces Scripture handwriting and explains why it is possibly the most powerful method of Bible meditation. Another addresses those who struggle to receive the love of God because of the pain they have experienced.

- Part One deals with the subject of Love in the New Testament. You'll learn the meaning of the nineteen Greek words translated as love and discover the Verse Concordance listing every form of the word love.

- Part Two covers the subject of Love in the Old Testament. Here you'll find the twenty-four Hebrew words rendered as some form of the word love and its concordance.

The book presents the New Testament part first (the opposite of normal Bible order) because it contains the words of Jesus, the Messiah.

The Word Sections

The Word Sections list each Greek or Hebrew word with: (1) its native alphabet; (2) pronunciation; (3) derivation, if known; (4) simple part of speech—noun, verb, adjective, etc.; (5) literal definition; (6) the Strong's Concordance number along with alternate spellings; and (7) the meaning and use of the word. The G or H before the Strong's number indicates Greek or Hebrew.

The *Translation Tally* catalogs every English word into which the original was rendered in *The New King James Version*, the number of times it was translated, and, in most cases, where to find each use.

When you turn to a Word Section, read the definition and commentary first. Scan the Translation Tally for an overview of how often the original word was translated as various English words. *Identify which English word (or words) most frequently translates the original.* As you meditate through the verses in *You and God*, try substituting the most common meaning in that verse. As you do, you'll understand why the context sometimes required translators to use different English words. Compare other Bible versions to see how they translated the word in its context.

For advanced study, consult the Greek and Hebrew lexicons (dictionaries) found in your Bible software. If you don't have a handy Bible program, many are accessible online for free. Reference works are often keyed to the Strong's number, which is provided.

The Verse Concordances

For an unparalleled overview of the biblical subject of *love*, read the Verse Concordance for the Testament you desire to study.

The Verse Concordances offer the reader an advantage over printed concordances and some Bible software. All the verses about *love* are combined in an easy-to-use concordance for each Testament. Full verses are provided, unlike the single-line listings in printed concordances. These verse lists are the best available for getting acquainted with the biblical subject of love.

In the Verse Concordance, every form of the word *love* is highlighted in bold print. The original Greek or Hebrew word from which it was translated follows in brackets, as shown in the sample below from Matthew.

3:17   And suddenly a voice *came* from heaven, saying, "This is My **beloved [3. agapetos]**...Son, in whom I am well pleased."

Each Greek and Hebrew word translating any form of the word *love* has a simple number that corresponds to its Word Section. For example, to learn more about the word "beloved" in the verse above, go to the New Testament Word Section 3. Agapetos.

Knowing the Greek and Hebrew words is essential to a biblical understanding of love. Each conveys a particular shade of meaning. In English, *love* can mean anything from simple liking (I *love* ice cream) to the self-sacrificing love of God (*agape*). To find the precise meaning in a given verse, go to the associated Word Section.

An ellipsis (...) is inserted into the Verse Concordance before or after the boldfaced word for *love* to help the reader take a meditational pause. The Bible is not a book that you can speed read. The idea is to slow down and read the verse one word at a time. This gives the Holy Spirit time to speak it to your heart and you time to hear Him.

You and God

The *You and God* section is a list of verses for you to hand copy. It includes every verse where the original word is translated as a form of the word love. A suggested context of a few verses follows the verse numbers in parentheses. For example, if the subject word occurs in verse 16, then a typical context might be verses 15 through 17. Studying the verse in its context always gives you a better understanding.

The idea of hand copying Scripture may be new to you, but it's more than a brain-dead, rote exercise, as you'll soon see. It will lead you to a heart-to-heart encounter with the living God through His Word.

The New King James Version

The New King James Version was chosen for the text of *Every Bible Verse on Love* because of its readability, reliability, and faithfulness to the original languages.

Though the amount of detail included may sound overwhelming, it's really not. The Holy Spirit has a lesson waiting for you as you become familiar with each original word and how it's used.

You may wish to read first what you're most interested in learning. Likewise, you can read thoroughly from beginning to end. You'll discover what works best for you. You may be pleasantly surprised by what you learn from the more obscure words.

As you read, study, and meditate, you are learning from the Book of books, the Bible, and being filled with the timeless wisdom of the ages. Learning to walk in the love of God, like Jesus did, is the most noble of pursuits. So, invest well in this your spiritual education. It will pay rich dividends.

EXPERIENCING GOD'S LOVE FOR THE FIRST TIME

Some of you may be drawn to this book because its subject is *love*. Perhaps, you have searched for love, been frustrated, and wonder if the Bible may say something to encourage you. For others, life has dealt you cruel blows. Maybe you've put yourself out there in love and ended up wounded and bleeding inside.

The healing love you hunger for originates in the heart of God. God's love is gentle, kind, unconditional, consistent, and accepts you just as you are. He is aware of your imperfections and loves and welcomes you just the same.

> For I know the thoughts that I think toward you, says the LORD, thoughts of peace and not of evil, to give you a future and a hope. Then you will call upon Me and go and pray to Me, and I will listen to you. And you will seek Me and find Me, when you search for Me with all your heart. —Jeremiah 29:11–13

> The LORD has appeared of old to me, saying: "Yes, I have loved you with an everlasting love; therefore with lovingkindness I have drawn you. Again I will build you, and you shall be rebuilt..." —Jeremiah 31:3–4a

> "I will betroth you to Me forever; Yes, I will betroth you to Me in righteousness and justice, in lovingkindness and mercy; I will betroth you to Me in faithfulness, and you shall know the LORD." —Hosea 2:19–20

Sometimes, people come to God because they are down and out. Others, however, may not be broken or depressed, but know instinctively something spiritual is missing from their life. You may be successful in your natural life and career. You may have achieved almost everything you ever wanted, but on the inside there is still a spiritual emptiness that success, money, possessions, and recreation cannot fulfill. Without a relationship with God, you subconsciously know that something isn't quite right.

Only the Lord can fill the God-shaped vacuum He designed into every human heart. He will overflow you with a good Father's love and give you the wholeness only He can give.

The way for anyone to experience the richness of God's love, no matter who you are or what you've done, is through His gift of Jesus.

> "For God so loved the world that He gave His only begotten Son, that whoever believes in Him should not perish but have everlasting life. For God did not send His Son into the world to condemn the world, but that the world through Him might be saved." —John 3:16–17

Through Jesus, you can be introduced to the warm, non-judgmental love of the Father. As God wraps you in His arms, He heals you of past wounds, delivers you from guilt, and causes you to experience the peace that passes all understanding. Jesus said,

> "I am the Way, the Truth, and the Life. No one comes to the Father except through Me." —John 14:6

As God draws you to Himself through Jesus, He forgives your past, heals your hurts and shattered dreams, and restores hope for your future. He takes those places of barrenness in your heart and fills them with His love. He reveals to you the true purpose for which you were created. It's something good you will love to do that calls on every talent God gave you.

If you would like to experience the forgiveness and love of God, I invite you to pray this prayer from your heart:

> *Father, I come to you just as I am. You know where I'm strong and where I'm broken and weak. You know my successes and my failures. You've seen my generosity and my selfishness. I confess that I've hurt others and made mistakes in life. Please forgive my sins and cleanse my conscience from guilt. Lord Jesus, I receive you now as my Savior. Thank you for dying on the cross, being raised from the dead, and making me right with God. Come into my heart, make me a new creation, give me a new nature, and fill me with Your Holy Spirit. Mend my broken wings and cause me to fly again, this time with You. In Jesus' name, I pray. Amen.*

If you prayed this prayer sincerely, God heard you. While you were praying, He caused you to be "born again." (John 3:1–8, 1 Peter 1:23–2:3) He has forgiven your sins and will never bring them up again. (Heb. 8:12, Rom. 8:1, ESV) You have peace with God through Jesus. (Rom. 5:1) Nothing in your past can ever separate you from God. (Rom. 8:38–39) His presence is with you now, strengthening and reassuring you of His love. God promises to never leave you nor forsake you. (Matt. 28:20, Heb. 13:5–6, Isa. 41:10, 43:2)

It's important to share with someone that you accepted Jesus as your Savior. Find a church that believes God's Word and knows the power of the Holy Spirit. You will be encouraged by other believers and learn the principles of God's kingdom. Read your Bible daily and study materials such as this book, and you will be spiritually "transformed by the renewing of your mind." (Rom. 12:1–2)

One Unusual Experience of God's Love

Receiving Christ as Savior means we become God's children, and He becomes our spiritual Father. Sometimes, He immerses His children in His love. God has ministered to me in various ways, but one time I felt the love of God directly.

About a year after accepting Jesus, I had driven for hours and was tired. We changed drivers, and I crawled into the back of the van to lie down. I slept a while and awakened to God's loving presence in and around me.

Having dealt with rejection when younger, His unconditional peace and acceptance was deeply reassuring. For several minutes, I basked in the warmth of this God-given security. But then something began to bother me.

God was making me feel as if I were His only son and favorite child. At first, I enjoyed it. Who doesn't want to be God's favorite? But then I felt guilty, knowing He has so many other beloved children. (God shows no partiality to anyone. Rom. 2:11) I finally protested, "This is not right. I know you love everyone as much as me."

Silently and quietly, He kept loving me as if I were His only child. After a few more minutes, His loving presence gently lifted. Though grateful and refreshed, I had unanswered questions.

Years later, I found the answer in Jesus' high priestly prayer of John 17.

"O righteous Father! The world has not known You, but I have known You; and these have known that You sent Me. And I have declared to them Your name, and will declare it, *that the love with which You loved Me may be in them, and I in them.*" —John 17:25–26 (italics added)

Then, I saw it! Jesus is in us, and we are in Him. (John 17:22–23, 1 Cor. 6:17) The love the Father has for Jesus is in us as well. In the van that day, I felt the love the Father has for His only begotten Son, who resides in me and all His believing children. We are all God's favorite child, because His favorite Son lives in each of us. God loves Jesus, Jesus is in us, so God loves us like He loves Jesus!

Though I felt His love for a few moments, John 17:26 is true whether we consciously experience His love in this life or the next. Spiritual experiences can be wonderful, but we must make sure they line up with the Word. How amazing it is when they actually help us understand the Word!

If you hunger for more of God's love, ask the Father in Jesus' name to reveal it to you. (John 14:21, 23) Pursue Him by listening to and obeying His instruction. As you seek first His kingdom and righteousness, all these things will be added to you. (Matt. 6:33) Don't seek experiences for the experience' sake. Ask, and then forget it. He hears you when you pray, so trust Him to surprise you when He is ready.

Remember, God is not mad at you. He loves you who for you are now, fully reconciled to Him by the sacrifice of Christ. Your sins are forgiven and forgotten, and God will never bring them up again. What a relief to know that you are a new creation in Christ and have turned over a fresh, new page! (2 Cor. 5:17) Your best times are ahead. Plus, you have a divine purpose and calling which draws on all the spiritual gifts and talents the Lord has birthed in you.

By receiving Jesus as your Savior, you became eligible to experience the love, grace, and soul peace that come only from the living God. World religions say many things about how to please their many "gods." But by *believing* in Christ, you receive the assurance you are forgiven and accepted by a real and knowable Person, a heavenly Father, whose love you can encounter for yourself.

IS LOVE GROWING COLD?

Jesus said of these last days, "And because lawlessness will abound, the love of many will grow cold." (Matthew 24:12) That doesn't have to describe you! When the culture trends toward hate, strife, and lawlessness, Jesus commands us to walk in love.

> "A new commandment I give to you, that you love one another; as I have loved you, that you also love one another. By this all will know that you are My disciples, if you have love for one another." —John 13:34–35

Walking in the self-sacrificing love of God is not normal or natural—it's supernatural! To operate in God's love, you must be radically, inwardly changed. Paul taught that we are transformed *only* by the renewing of our minds. (Romans 12:2) Renewing the mind means learning to think as Jesus thinks from reading God's book, the Bible. Transformed hearts act with love!

This book is designed to help you renew your mind in the area of divine love. The exercises are reading, studying, meditating, and hand copying Scriptures. You may think, *I'm too busy for that.* If you are too busy for God, then you are *too busy.* Rethink your priorities. Delegate. Let some things go. Whether you are a fast-paced, driven executive or a single mom doing everything on your own, carve out time for God. As we'll soon see, God commanded even the busiest kings of Israel to handwrite two copies of the law.

Changing is hard. You can't modify deep-seated attitudes and behavior by skimming a little of the Bible now and then. When you sit down to God's Word, eat a nutritious meal. Give the Holy Spirit a chance to speak into your life. Like food, the thoughts of God must be chewed, swallowed, and absorbed before they supply any nutrients. Slow down, take a breath, and think about what you're reading. Hand copying Scripture is the best method I know for meditating in God's Word. But your *spiritual hunger* for God must convince your mind and flesh to do it. (Matt. 5:6)

When you said Yes to Jesus, *God* re-created your spirit. (Eph. 4:24, 1 Thess. 5:23) The Bible calls that being born again. But it's *your* job to renew your soul—your mind, will, and emotions. You are to put off the old worldly thoughts and put on new and Christlike thoughts from God's Word. God won't renew your mind for you, but His Holy Spirit will help if you make the effort. Will you say Yes to Him today and commit to a daily devotional time?

Father, I will not let my love grow cold. I have determined to set a regular appointment with You, the most important Person in my life. I will do whatever it takes to rearrange my schedule and set aside time for You when my mind is fresh. I desire to be transformed by the renewing my mind, to think as Jesus thinks, and to love as He loves. So, help me make time for You. Holy Spirit, open my understanding as I read the Bible. Coach me to apply it to my life and walk in Christlike love. In Jesus' name, I pray. Amen.

IT'S ALL ABOUT THE WORD

A church member summed up my teaching on the importance of Bible reading in a sentence, "The way we show our love for God is by reading His Word." Bible reading is truly loving God with our hearts and minds.

The patriarch Job would have loved to have the dust-covered Bibles we take for granted. He hungered to understand life from God's perspective. At one point, he cried, "Oh, that the Almighty would answer me, that my Prosecutor had written a book! Surely I would carry it on my shoulder, and bind it on me like a crown." (Job 31:35a–36) What a privilege to have access to God's Word, so we can understand His ways!

But having the book Job longed for, do we read it? Do we desire the knowledge of God like Job did? Does our love for God's truth make us set aside time to grow in Christ? Are we willing to forego temporal pleasures for eternal truth? Have we established the wonderful habit of reading God's Word daily? Someone said it well: We form habits, then habits form us.

The Bible spells out the invaluable benefits of meditating daily in the Scriptures, including success (through God's wisdom), continual refreshing, freedom, holiness, patience, comfort, hope, spiritual transformation, and complete equipping for every good work, to mention a few.

> "This Book of the Law shall not depart from your mouth, but you shall *meditate in it day and night,* that you may observe to do according to all that is written in it. For then you will make your way prosperous, and then you will have good success." —Joshua 1:8 (italics added)

> Blessed is the man
> Who walks not in the counsel of the ungodly,
> Nor stands in the path of sinners,
> Nor sits in the seat of the scornful;

But his delight is in the law of the LORD,
And in His law he meditates day and night.
He shall be like a tree planted by the rivers of water,
That brings forth its fruit in its season,
Whose leaf also shall not wither;
And whatever he does shall prosper. —Psalms 1:1–3 (italics added)

Oh, how I love Your law!
It is my meditation all the day.
You, through Your commandments, make me wiser than my enemies;
For they are ever with me.
I have more understanding than all my teachers,
For Your testimonies are my meditation.
I understand more than the ancients,
Because I keep Your precepts. —Psalms 119:97–100 (italics added)

Remember *the word* to Your servant,
Upon which You have caused me to hope.
This is my comfort in my affliction,
For Your word has given me life. —Psalms 119:49–50 (italics added)

Then Jesus said to those Jews who believed Him, "*If you abide* [remain, continue, dwell, make your home] *in My word, you are My disciples indeed. And you shall know the truth, and the truth shall make you free.*" —John 8:31–32 (italics added)

"*Sanctify them by Your truth. Your word is truth.*" —John 17:17 (italics added)

These were *more fair-minded* than those in Thessalonica, in that *they received the word with all readiness, and searched the Scriptures daily* to find out whether these things were so. —Acts 17:11 (italics added)

For whatever things were written before were written *for our learning, that we through the patience and comfort of the Scriptures might have hope.* —Romans 15:4 (italics added)

I beseech you therefore, brethren, by the mercies of God, that you present your bodies a living sacrifice, holy, acceptable to God, which is your reasonable service. *And do not be conformed to this world, but be transformed by the renewing of your mind,* that you may prove what is that good and acceptable and perfect will of God. —Romans 12:1–2 (italics added)

But we all, with unveiled face, *beholding as in a mirror* [God's Word] *the glory of the Lord, are being transformed into the same image* from glory to glory, just as by the Spirit of the Lord. —2 Corinthians 3:18 (italics added)

Till I come, *give attention to reading, to exhortation, to doctrine.* Do not neglect the gift that is in you, which was given to you by prophecy with the laying on of the hands of the eldership. *Meditate on these things; give yourself entirely to them, that your progress may be evident to all. Take heed to yourself and to the doctrine. Continue in them, for in doing this you will save both yourself and those who hear you.* —1 Timothy 4:13–16 (italics added)

But you must continue in the things which you have learned and been assured of, knowing from whom you have learned them, and that from childhood you have known *the Holy Scriptures, which are able to make you wise for salvation through faith which is in Christ Jesus. All Scripture is given by inspiration of God, and is profitable for doctrine, for reproof, for correction, for instruction in righteousness, that the man of God may be complete, thoroughly equipped for every good work.* —2 Timothy 3:14–17 (italics added)

Every Bible Verse on Love supports you, the reader, in your quest to meditate in the Word of God. By taking a single subject, such as *love*, and tracing it through the Bible, you will see things in Scripture you've never seen before. As you apply what you learn, the Word will work its way from the inside out to your attitudes and behavior. And that will improve your love walk, increasing your favor with God and men.

Nothing pleases the Father more than to see those who hear the Word become doers of the Word. Obedience is the most accurate test of discipleship. Jesus said it simply, "If you love Me, keep My commandments." (John 14:15) Meditate in the Word. Obey the Word. It will bring you the blessings of deep peace and godly success.

You don't have to be a rocket scientist to read and understand God's Word. Ask the Holy Spirit, who knows all things, to teach you, line upon line, precept upon precept. Others will be amazed and helped by what He shows you.

WHY A TOPICAL WORD STUDY?

One could compare the Bible to a rare and priceless tapestry hanging on the wall of a great room in a museum. This richly woven masterpiece is a hundred feet long. As people step into the room and gaze at it in silent awe, slowly walking its length, they are thrilled by the impressive skill of the Weaver. Using thousands of threads, He has embroidered a full-color portrayal of God's dealings with man, ultimately highlighting the sacrifice and resurrection of the Savior, Jesus Christ.

But suppose someone pulled from the tapestry all the horizontal threads and left only the vertical ones. Half of the masterpiece would have been destroyed, devastating the viewer. Or suppose someone removed all the vertical threads and left just the horizontal strands. That, too, would ruin the fullness of God's picture.

We can liken the vertical threads of God's woven work, the Bible, to the chronological events the Bible records. Every vertical strand has its place where it crosses the timeline of history that travels the tapestry's length. The long horizontal threads are the grand topics, themes, and words of the Bible, traceable from Genesis to Revelation.

When we study the Bible only from a historical perspective, we single out the vertical threads of the key events recorded in the Bible. In so doing, we overlook the rich beauty of the thematical. If we study only great Bible themes and topics, we lose track of the historical events and people that gave those themes significance and relevance.

We have to consider the whole counsel of God, both warp and woof, both historical and thematical, to appreciate the complete picture. In the Bible, God gave us a tightly woven, integrated whole that defies study in only one direction. We find extraordinary riches in what God did through individuals in their historical settings. We uncover equally glorious treasures by tracing a theme, such as love, throughout God's Word.

Study Bibles often incorporate both approaches. Book introductions and verse notes convey vital information about who the author was, the time in which he wrote, and the historical and cultural background. Topical study chains and other aids track important passages on critical themes.

Every Bible Verse on Love is a *topical* study. Its purpose is to trace the remarkable subject of *love* from Genesis to Revelation. The reader will be blessed by what he finds but is cautioned to be mindful of the historical context and setting of each verse.

SCRIPTURE HANDWRITING AND ENGAGING YOUR BRAIN

I can't convey to you what a rich method of meditation Scripture handwriting is. I can only challenge you to find out for yourself. Each Word Section contains a list of verses called *You and God*. I invite you to hand copy these verses from your Bible with the indicated contexts. Hand copying requires time and effort, and that makes this a *workbook*.

By studying these verses in their contexts, you discover the unique essence of each Greek or Hebrew word. Every word in the original languages is a subject in itself. Jesus said, "It is written, 'Man shall not live by bread alone, but by *every word* that proceeds from the mouth of God.' " (Matt. 4:4) Are you willing to become a *Word person*?

After hand writing for a time, you may discover that God whispers to you as you copy. Treasure His thoughts. (Ps. 139:17–18) Write in a journal or notebook what you think He is saying. You'll find His thoughts about you are higher and better than your thoughts about yourself. (Isa. 55:8–11, Jer. 29:11–12) Meditating in God's Word reveals *who you are in Christ,* frees you from the past, and inspires you to press toward the future with joy and anticipation.

God Required Kings to Hand Copy His Word

God believed hand copying was so helpful that *He commanded the kings of Israel to do it!* He did not view this time-intensive practice as a misuse of the ruler's day but *as necessary to transform the leader's heart.*

The king was to write a copy of the law and read from it daily. He could not hire a scribe to do the writing for him.

"Also it shall be, when he sits on the throne of his kingdom, *that he shall write for himself a copy of this law in a book,* from the one before the priests, the

Levites. *And it shall be with him, and he shall read it all the days of his life*, that he may learn to fear the LORD his God and be careful to observe all the words of this law and these statutes, that his heart may not be lifted above his brethren, that he may not turn aside from the commandment to the right hand or to the left, and that he may prolong his days in his kingdom, he and his children in the midst of Israel." —Deuteronomy 17:18–20 (italics added)

Interestingly, the Chumash translates the passage like this: "…he shall write for himself *two copies* of this Torah in a book…" The king was to keep one copy with him at all times so he could read from it. The second was to be placed in his treasury, so he would not be blinded by his wealth and forget he was the servant of God.[1]

The good kings in Israel appear to have done what God required. The bad kings? Probably not. But I'm sure they had "important kingly things" to do that kept them out of the light-filled Word. That meant they continued thinking the thoughts of ego, pride, and indulgence according to this world's present darkness. Their refusal also hindered them from making godly decisions when it mattered most to their nation.

King Hezekiah benefited so much from handwriting the Word that he ordered his men to copy King Solomon's proverbs. Hezekiah, through his changed heart, led a spiritual revival that restored his nation's spiritual life. (2 Chron. 29–32) It's likely that his princes and ministers of state copied Proverbs 25–29 to learn how to conduct themselves properly in the king's court.

> These also are proverbs of Solomon which the men of Hezekiah king of Judah *copied*:
>
> It is the glory of God to conceal a matter,
> But the glory of kings is to search out a matter. —Proverbs 25:1–2 (italics added)

We Are "Kings and Priests"

God calls *us* "kings and priests" in Christ, so shouldn't the same requirement apply? (Rev. 1:6) We reign as kings in life through an abundance of grace and a transformed heart. (Rom. 5:17, 21) But unless we, too, renew our minds through Scripture, our decisions will suffer.

Jesus spoke of *Christian "scribes"* who would find treasures in the Word of God.

> Then He said to them, "Therefore every *scribe* instructed concerning the kingdom of heaven is like a householder who brings out of his *treasure* things new and old." —Matthew 13:52 (italics added)

---

[1] Rabbi Nosson Scherman and Rabbi Meir Zlotowitz, Gen. Eds., *The Chumash*, Artscroll/Stone Edition, 11th Ed. (Brooklyn: Mesorah Publications, Ltd., 2012), p. 1029.

Jesus wasn't referring to the professional Jewish scribes who copied Old Testament scrolls with letter-for-letter accuracy. He foresaw "householders" and "scribes," everyday Christians who prayerfully copied the Scriptures and received the Holy Spirit's life-changing instructions. These Christian kings and priests uncover liberating truths, new and old, from the treasures of the Bible.

Seven Benefits of Hand Copying Scripture

Hand copying Scripture has many benefits.

- *It is humbling.* Some brothers and sisters don't read or write and must humble themselves to learn how. Others don't have nice handwriting. Plus, when someone doesn't understand the passage they're copying, they have to ask someone who does. If other people find out you are copying Scripture, they may jump to judgment and accuse you of wasting your time. Just tell them, "Hand copying Scripture is the meditation practiced by kings. I intend to reign in life, and the Bible is teaching me how to do it."

- *It requires sacrifice.* The king had to restructure his royal lifestyle to make time for God and copying the Scriptures.

- *It brings the copyist under the influence of the Holy Spirit.* The Holy Spirit guides those who meditate in God's Word, giving them wisdom beyond their years.

- *It follows the first commandment.* You are commanded to love God with all your heart, soul, *mind,* and strength. How do you love God with your mind? When you meditate in His Word.

- *It is healing.* I received healing from a brain concussion while copying Scripture, and others have received healing as well. (Prov. 4:20–22)

- *It improves your mind.* Hand copying quiets your mind and trains it to concentrate on one thing at a time, free from distracting thoughts. A quieted mind empowers you to do things better, including praying, hearing God's voice, learning new skills, and receiving creative ideas.

- *It draws you closer to God.* When you abide (make your home) in God's Word, God's presence draws near in tangible ways, bringing joy to your heart.

Let's talk more about some of these benefits.

Engaging More of Your Brain

In simple reading, you use your brain's visual and verbal areas. When you hand copy Scripture, you stimulate more of it than in reading only.

Hand copying uses the parts of the brain that control vision, memory, motor skills, and speech. First, your *eyes* read a phrase from the text you are copying. Your *memory* stores it. Then your *hand* writes it down, requiring eye-hand coordination. You are likely to *speak* it under your breath as you copy it. Some people find they *memorize* the verses by writing them out.

This simple but complex process gives your spirit more time to listen to the Holy Spirit than in reading alone. It helps you better digest and absorb the truth. An added benefit is hearing God whispering "between the lines," counseling you regarding your personal life.

Healing Through the Word

After the oil rig accident, I suffered the aftereffects of a concussion. I had headaches, sensitivity to noise, nightmares, and an impaired ability to think clearly and make decisions. Hand copying Scriptures four hours a day was my pathway to healing.

Doing this was a challenge. Some days I had to force myself to do it, but through it all, I received a healing that restored my physical and mental capacities. Because the practice helped quiet my mind, it improved my ability to concentrate and learn new things.

Handwriting for hours was more difficult than I thought it would be. At first, my right arm was in a sling due to the shoulder injury. I'm right-handed and not particularly ambidextrous, but I started out writing with my left hand. If you've ever tried using the other hand, it's as awkward as learning to write all over again. But soon, I was able to switch back to my right hand.

I fought boredom and wandering thoughts. I wasn't accustomed to a steady diet of God's Word. When my mind wandered, I returned it to the verse at hand. A few times, when I could not stay awake, I fell asleep with my face on my hands. When I awoke, I would continue.

At times, frustration, even anger, arose at having to do this. Some days I complained and felt sorry for myself. But I kept writing until those feelings left and God's peace returned. It was a toughening, cleansing, spiritual "boot camp" experience. Through persistence, I drove away the spiritual forces that opposed my learning God's Word.

On other days, I would be refreshed as the Spirit of God came over me and filled me with His love, peace, and life. While writing, the Holy Spirit often gave me Bible insights. He also reminded me of natural things I needed to do that I had forgotten, showed me how to solve problems, or inspired me to begin a new project or task. Because of the wisdom God gave me while I copied, I wasted less time and came out further ahead in my day than if I didn't study. He does the same things today.

My normal thought functions were restored quickly, but it took a few years for the headaches and sensitivity to noise to leave. But I thank God for showing me how to quiet my mind and draw His life, strength, and healing from Scripture handwriting.

> My son, give attention to my words;
> Incline your ear to my sayings.
> Do not let them depart from your eyes;
> Keep them in the midst of your heart;
> For they are *life* to those who find them,
> And *health* to all their flesh. —Proverbs 4:20–22 (italics added)

After sharing my testimony in a church, a young lady told me her story. At age seventeen, she became paralyzed by what I believe was a stroke. All she could move were her eyes. Her mother tried to get her to watch television, but she couldn't. Reading the Bible was the only thing that helped.

At first, her mother had to turn the pages for her. But as she read, the paralysis began to leave. The more she read, the faster it went. When I met her a couple of years later, she seemed perfectly normal. She was on the worship team, and I would never have guessed she had been paralyzed. There is power in the Word of God!

Improving Your Mind

A significant benefit of Scripture handwriting is training your mind to be quiet and to focus. An untrained mind is a tangled briar patch of random thoughts. We all need to cultivate the skill of tuning out distracting thoughts. Hand copying Scripture is a powerful tool toward this end. The more you discipline your mind to stay focused on God, the more you enter His peace.

The Bible tells us in Romans 8:6, "For to be carnally minded is death, but to be spiritually minded is life and peace." What better way to enter God's peace than to train yourself to be spiritually minded through writing Scripture! (Phil. 4:6–9) You not only enjoy peace, but you renew your mind as well.

Here's how to train your mind. *Focus* your mental energies and *concentrate* one hundred percent on each word from God. If your mind wanders off like a straying calf, lasso it, and bring it back. After disciplining your mind like this for a while, your ability to concentrate will noticeably improve. We train our pets; why not our minds?

The more you quiet your mind before the Lord, the easier it is for you to discern His still, small voice, be guided by His wisdom, and be refreshed in His presence. Scripture handwriting increases your ability to pray free from distracting thoughts. Training your mind to take every thought captive is at the heart of spiritual warfare. (2 Cor. 10:5)

Improving your concentration pays dividends in every area of life, not just prayer. It enhances your ability to think clearly and helps greatly in learning new skills, making you more effective at work and in life. It teaches you to receive God's inspiration, resulting in greater creativity.

Everyone should prayerfully seek the inspiration of God. A new idea can be worth millions in the business world. It could result in favor with your company, a promotion, better income, or starting a business and becoming your own boss. Through God's wisdom, you become a better parent, spouse, or worker at church.

This book would not exist without the time I spent writing God's Word. I wrote it out by hand several times. Once, I typed it on a 1917 Underwood typewriter out of someone's garage. I retyped it on an electronic typewriter with changeable font wheels. When I got a computer, I typed it into a word processor, using a Bible program to paste in the Scriptures. Then I typeset it in a book publishing program. You hold the third edition of the typeset version.

Do I know everything God wants me to learn about love? No! But I learn something valuable every time I return to the subject. Has it changed my life for the better? Absolutely! Am I perfect? No, for the Bible word *love* has more to speak into my life.

To this day, whenever I have the chance, I like to copy parts of the New Testament or write out topical Word studies like this one. The Spirit of God comes over me with remarkable grace and wisdom whenever I do.

I encourage you to use the *You and God* Scriptures to join with the Holy Spirit in Scripture meditation. Take the time to handwrite every verse and context from your own Bible. Become a *Word person*. Get into the Word, and allow what God says about *love* to get into you.

Jesus said in John 15:7, "If you abide in Me, and My words abide in you, you will ask what you desire, and it shall be done for you." There's no better Word to fill the treasure chest of your heart with than this one! Be an imitator of Christ. Do your best to walk in God's love!

RENEWING YOUR MIND REQUIRES PRAYER

The apostle Paul taught in Romans 12:2, "And do not be conformed to this world, but *be transformed by the renewing of your mind…*" Renewing your mind means learning from the Bible how to think as God thinks. The key to spiritual growth is filling your mind with the thoughts of God. We are to put off the world's way of thinking and put on the mind of Christ. (1 Cor. 2:16, Phil. 2:5, 1 Peter 2:2)

The word "transformed" comes from an interesting Greek word, *metamorphoo* (Strong's G3339). Our English word *metamorphosis* is derived from it. As you probably know, metamorphosis is the process by which a creeping, crawling, leaf-munching caterpillar transforms into a beautiful, flying butterfly. Its *transformation* allows it to defy the gravity that once held it earthbound.

Similarly, a dramatic transformation happens in us spiritually *when we renew our minds in God's Word!* We are changed from an earthly-minded, crawling, baby Christian to a heavenly-minded, mature Christian. But this happens only if we consume the Word of God! Then, and only then, will we be able to soar like a spiritual eagle born aloft on the wings of the Holy Spirit.

Begin with Prayer

You cannot accelerate your spiritual growth and transformation any faster than you are willing to renew your mind. That is why God tells you to meditate in His Word "day and night." Bible meditation turns you into an on-fire, growing Christian, able to share Christ with others. (John 8:31, Josh. 1:8, Ps. 1:2) "Day and night" means "morning and evening." God wants us to meditate in Scripture in the morning when our mind is fresh and at night before we sleep. (We'll have more peace and sleep better.)

Your mind is not renewed until you are *acting* on the Word. So, invite the Holy Spirit to take the Word and illuminate it to your heart. When it makes sense, you become *willing* to do it. Jesus is looking for doers of the Word, not hearers only. (Matt. 7:24–27, James 1:22–25)

The Holy Spirit is your guide into all truth (John 16:13), but He moves in response to your prayers and hunger for God. If you want to grow, pray for the Holy Spirit to make the Bible "living and powerful" in you. (Heb. 4:12) When the Word comes alive, you understand it, are convinced of its truth, and are willing to live it. *Prayerful* reading and Spirit-led study is your assignment. Begin your daily devotional time with prayer for God's overshadowing wisdom and insight.

In his epistles, the apostle Paul left us powerful prayers. If you *personalize* these, making them your own, your Bible study time will never be the same. Personalizing means inserting your name wherever Paul says "you" or "your." May the Holy Spirit give *you* the spirit of wisdom and revelation in the knowledge of Him.

Sample Prayers

Father, I pray that You, the God of our Lord Jesus Christ, the Father of glory, may give to *me* (*your name*) the spirit of wisdom and revelation in the knowledge of You, the eyes of *my* understanding being enlightened; that *I* may know what is the hope of Your calling, what are the riches of the glory of Your inheritance in *me*, and what is the exceeding greatness of Your power toward *me* who believes. (Adapted from Eph. 1:17–19)

Father, I ask that *I* (*your name*) may be filled with the knowledge of Your will in all wisdom and spiritual understanding; that *I* may walk worthy of the Lord, fully pleasing You, being fruitful in every good work and increasing in the knowledge of God; that *I* may be strengthened with all might, according to Your glorious power, for all patience and longsuffering with joy; giving thanks to You who have qualified *me* to be a partaker of the inheritance of the saints in light. (Adapted from Col. 1:9–12)

For this reason I bow my knees to the Father of our Lord Jesus Christ, from whom the whole family in heaven and earth is named, that He would grant *me* (*your name*) according to the riches of His glory, to be strengthened with might through His Spirit in *my* inner man, that Christ may dwell in *my* heart through faith; that *I*, being rooted and grounded in love, may be able to comprehend with all the saints what is the width and length and depth and height—to know the love of Christ which passes knowledge; that *I* may be filled with all the fullness of God. (Adapted from Eph. 3:14–19)

Holy Spirit, guide *me* into all truth. Take the things of Jesus and declare them to *me*, that *I* may know the things freely given to *me* by God. (Adapted from John 16:13–15 and 1 Cor. 2:12)

Open *my* eyes, that *I* may see wondrous things from Your law. (Ps. 119:18)

Lord, speak to *me* through Your Word.

Warning!

This book is not "fast food." It requires discipline on your part. Doing the Scripture handwriting will challenge you to train *your mind* to prayerful Bible study. Becoming rooted and grounded in love will test you to the deepest parts of your being and sift every motive of your heart!

Reading about what it means to walk in divine love is personally challenging. We love to hear of the unconditional love of God for us as individuals but discussing the *other-centered* aspects of divine love exposes our self-centeredness. It's painful to have God's Word illuminate our hearts only to reveal an ugly root of self-love lurking there.

When something hurts, we want to stop doing whatever causes the pain. Please don't stop reading. Remember, the definitions of divine love, especially *agape* and *agapao*, describe the "ideal." No one but Jesus ever met that standard. If you feel like you fall short, join the crowd. The fall of Adam corrupted humankind to the core. It takes rebirth, baptism, the Word of God, and the Spirit of God to lift us out of where we were and make us new creations walking in love.

So, please don't feel like a failure if you don't love perfectly. Receive God's forgiveness. You can't do this on your own. Trust God's grace to make you better. Allow the Helper (the Holy Spirit) to help you. It's necessary for the Word to expose where we are, so we know where we need to grow.

The effort is so rewarding. You'll be amazed at how you can succeed in loving difficult people. You'll sail through stormy tests that at one time would have swamped your boat. Further, as you meditate, digest, absorb, assimilate, and continue to act on the Word, God will lead you around the bend in your path to vistas of understanding you can't see from where you stand now. God has stored up treasures for you to discover along the way. But you will never find them unless you get in the Word, stay in the Word, and obey the Word.

> Then Jesus said to those Jews who believed Him, "If you *abide* [dwell, remain, continue, make your home] in My word, you are My disciples indeed. And you shall know the truth, and the truth shall make you free." —John 8:31–32 (italics added)

Every Bible Verse on Love puts you in touch with the primary source material—the pure Word of God—absolute, eternal, unchangeable, and incorruptible! In all the world, there is nothing to equal the undistilled Word of God. There is no brighter Light! (Isa. 8:20) As God's Word has transformed believers through the centuries, it will not fail to transform you.

HURT? WOUNDED? DISCOURAGED? FEEL LIKE GOD LET YOU DOWN?

People often struggle with the truth that God is love when terrible things have happened to them. They wonder where God has been in all they've suffered, and we're not talking about broken fingernails or flat tires. Many question, "If God is love, how could He cause, condone, or permit evil things to happen?" (The short answer is, He didn't!)

We tend to ask *why* devastating things happened to us and *why* He didn't prevent them. *Why* did that special loved one die for whom we prayed with all our heart? *Why* did our "forever" relationship fail? *What* did we do to deserve this? When we don't understand, we pull away from the Lord, especially if we think that He could have kept it from happening. Even if God didn't cause the bad stuff directly, we often think He "allowed" it, which doesn't make us feel any better.

As a result, many people are angry with God though not all confess it openly. (It sounds like blasphemy to be mad at Someone who is perfect, so it's hard to admit when we are.) But if you are mad at God, be honest about it. Have that conversation with Him. Tell Him exactly how you feel. I have and wasn't hit with lightning. The Lord has broad shoulders and can handle our intense feelings without turning away.

On one of the most challenging days of my life, I vented all my frustration to God, holding nothing back. Afterward, His peace came over me. He breathed wisdom into my soul and showed me how to handle the situation with grace. The Lord counted my outcry as prayer, for at least I directed my words to Him and not to the person who hurt me so deeply.

Until we deal properly with our pain, evil experiences damage our relationship with the Lord. It's like getting your car stuck in the mud. The more you spin the tires, the deeper you sink. The more questions you ask without clear answers, the more abandoned you feel. The Lord desires to help us out of the bog, so we can move forward in faith once again. So, please let me explain why your anger is misplaced if you are blaming God for the evil you suffered.

A book about love may be an odd place to address why bad things happen to good people. But with so many questioning God's love, I think it's appropriate. These hard questions drive a wedge between us and God. If we can't get past them, how can we receive His love? So, here goes.

The Assumption That Trips Up Most People

The idea that God is responsible for or "allows" evil is rooted in a popular *assumption* that sounds reasonable on the surface. Nevertheless, it contradicts Scripture. Assumptions are hard to unlearn because they slide into our minds without us giving them much thought.

We have heard that God is sovereign and all-powerful. He is! Having said that, here's where we jump to a conclusion. We automatically *assume* that because God is all-powerful that He must *micromanage* everything that happens on earth. Again, God *is* sovereign and all-powerful. But it's an *assumption* to suppose that everything that happens on earth is filtered through His will and given His stamp of approval.

Does God will for everyone to be saved? Yes. (John 3:16–17, 2 Pet. 3:9, Rom. 10:13, 9–10) He is not willing for any to perish. Salvation is God's will, but is everyone saved? No. Why? Because God's will is not always being done. For this reason, Jesus taught us to pray, "Your kingdom come, Your will be done on earth as in heaven." (Matt. 6:10) If God's will is always done, it's pointless to pray that way. But Jesus thought it necessary to pray for God's kingdom to come and His will to be done.

Who Did God Put in Charge of Earth?

In the beginning, God put *mankind* in charge of earth. He created Adam and Eve[2] in the image of God and chose to give them *dominion* and *free will*. (Gen. 1:26, 28)

---

[2] Adam and Eve were a historical couple. Genesis records the years of Adam's life, the names of his children, and his genealogy of descent. (Gen. 5:1–32) Jesus confirmed their existence as our original parents. (Matt. 19:4–5) Their narrative is not unique to the Bible. It is embedded in cultures worldwide in the earliest stories passed down through the generations. The names and details vary but the story of a first couple being deceived by a "trickster" is intact in a surprising number of places. The account preserved by the Karen people of Myanmar (Burma) and Thailand is nearly identical to the Bible's record. It existed centuries prior to the coming of missionaries. A well-documented and fascinating report of the Karen's spiritual tradition and rapid conversion to Christianity is found in Don Richardson's book, *Eternity in Their Hearts*, published by Regal Books, 1984, pp. 78–80. The Karen's original name for God was Y'wa (cp. the Hebrew, *Yahweh*). Their elders taught that old age, sickness, and death came from the first two being deceived into eating fruit from the wrong tree. Richardson also records the account of the Santal people of India who knew of the "Genuine God" even though the people began to worship the sun. Their sages told of our first parents and the deception that took place in a land far to the west of them. They describe the difficulties of their people's migration from the Middle East across the Himalayas into India. (*Eternity in Their Hearts*, pp. 41–44) Native North Americans also describe the "trickster" (Coyote, Raven) duping our original parents. Other traditions around the world narrate a similar story of a first couple, deception, disobedience, and loss of Paradise. There are too many similar accounts in

Dominion in Hebrew means *to rule, dominate, tread down, govern,* and *subdue.* God made Adam and Eve earth's rulers, and they and their children (us) were to rule under God and in communion with Him. (Gen. 2:15) In Psalm 8, David marveled that God would give mankind dominion over the work of His hands. (Psalm 8:3–8)

However, the Lord did not create Adam and Eve as robots programmed to obey Him. From the moment He granted our original parents free will, there was no guarantee that His will would be done on earth. They had the freedom to obey or to disobey.

> The heaven, even the heavens, are the LORD's;
> *But the earth He has given to the children of men.* —Psalm 115:16 (italics added)

This Scripture shocked me when I first read it literally. I had always assumed somewhere in the back of my mind that God controlled everything. The verse is, however, consistent with God's Word giving mankind dominion. God ceased to manage everything that happened on earth when He put humanity in charge. So, when we humans have a problem, we needn't blame God for the violence, war, and poverty. We need to look in the mirror. God is not responsible. We are!

These concepts may be new to some. There's a fuller explanation in my book, *The Armor of Light,* in Chapter 7, "Why You Must Pray." Here's a brief excerpt.

> Actually, the Bible never says that the Lord is "in control" but rather that the Lord *reigns.* For example, the king who reigns over a country does not control everything that happens in it, but everyone in the country is accountable to the king for their actions.[3]

When God spoke the words giving Adam and Eve dominion, He imposed limits on Himself. He no longer governed everything that happened because humanity was free to choose for themselves. If God foresaw an individual was about to make a bad decision, He predetermined not to intervene forcibly. People were free to choose and to live with the consequences of their choices, good or bad. If the Lord used His mighty power to override their decisions, then His Word giving them dominion and freedom of choice would be a *lie.*

But God is truth Himself, and lying is one thing even the sovereign God cannot do. Because He cannot lie, *God's Word is the expression of His sovereignty.* (Titus 1:2) Once spoken, He will not change or alter it.

---

diverse parts of the globe to be coincidental, and they confirm the Bible's record. Even the scientific study of mitochondrial DNA indicates we all descended from one woman, Eve. I don't doubt the Bible's account and look forward to meeting Adam and Eve one day in heaven.

[3] Michael Christian, *The Armor of Light,* Twin Pillars Press, Paradise, CA, pp. 67–68.

> "God is not a man, that He should lie,
> Nor a son of man, that He should repent.
> Has He said, and will He not do?
> Or has He spoken, and will He not make it good?" —Numbers 23:19

> "My covenant I will not break,
> Nor alter the word that has gone out of My lips." —Psalm 89:34

God's sovereignty is expressed through His Word, and He will not violate what He has spoken. (Matt. 24:35, John 12:46–50) When you want to know what the Lord will or will not do on the earth, you'll find it in His Word.

Having given humanity dominion in the beginning, God did *not* later in history take back control. He influences, instructs, and counsels mankind to do good. But for His Word's sake, He does not (normally) intervene directly.

We see an example of how God works in the account of Cain and Abel. (Gen. 4:6–8) God saw that Cain was jealous enough to kill his brother and commit the first murder. So, the Lord spoke to Cain and counseled him to control his anger. Unfortunately, Cain ignored God and murdered his brother. *God did not send an angel to restrain him although He knew murder was in Cain's heart.*

Don't get me wrong. The Lord does everything He can to speak to, counsel, and influence people *not* to do evil, but the choice is theirs. Since He gave mankind dominion, God must intervene through people. He inspires *others* to come alongside troubled individuals and talk them out of the evil they imagine. He uses people to thwart their evil plans if they are known.

The Lord warns us of potential danger through His still small voice, hunches, intuitions, impressions, dreams, and "red flags" about certain individuals. He attempts to move people out of the reach of those who intend to do them harm. Of course, it makes a difference if we are listening for His voice and sensitive to His impressions.

Before you went through your trials, the Lord did His best to warn you and ask someone to intervene on your behalf. He desired to prevent the evil that happened to you, me, and billions of others. But people don't always hear, obey, or cooperate with the Lord's voice.

Here's the point: *God did not grant permission to the evil that you and I suffered at the hands of others.* He didn't plan, authorize, or condone it. It was caused by the free will choices of those who hurt us. God "allows" evil only in the sense that He created mankind in His image with freedom of choice, but He is not responsible for the way we choose to use or abuse that freedom.

Of course, He could solve the problem of evil in one day by removing our free will and turning us into robots programmed to do His will. But then, we would no longer be made in the image of God, and our love would be mechanical rather than freely given.

If we are honest, we've also brought pain and difficulty on ourselves as the consequences of our freely willed but unenlightened decisions. Plus, we live in a fallen world containing sickness and disease, aging, death, accidents, and destructive forces of nature such as hurricanes, tornadoes, and wildfires.

For example, I live in Paradise, California. Our town was almost completely destroyed by wildfire in 2018, and eighty-five people lost their lives. But I don't blame God for this tragedy. It was a perfect storm of dry conditions, high winds, and sparks caused by a poorly maintained utility line.

How Does God Intervene?

Fortunately, God desires to bring His protection into our lives to defend us from evildoers.[4] But it requires an action on our part. Because the Lord gave humanity dominion, most things that happen on earth must be *initiated* by a human. (Even redemption had to be accomplished by One born of a woman, who was *fully Man* as well as fully God—Jesus.)

That's why prayer is not just a good idea—it is necessary! Prayer is that unique event that brings together the free will of man and the sovereign power of God. When you call on the Lord for help, He begins moving on your behalf through the spiritual channels He has reserved for Himself.

But if you don't pray, He can't move. He has the power, but you have the dominion. You must initiate God's intervention by asking for it. (James 4:3, Matt. 7:7–8) He won't intervene without your request because He is a perfect gentleman and doesn't impose His will over your free will. (God's grace helps at times when we haven't prayed because of the prayers of Jesus and others who intercede for us.)

When you ask in prayer, God begins to cause all things to work together for your good. (Rom. 8:26–28) He gives you grace and favor with people and guides your steps with His wisdom.

But please, don't get stuck in the fruitless loop where you're waiting for God to move, and He's waiting for you to pray. It's *after* we have prayed and put the situation in God's hands that we can assure ourselves He is making all things work together for our good. After prayer, we can boldly confess that God is "in control."

---

[4] Divine protection is a covenant blessing. We enter the covenant by accepting Jesus Christ as our Lord and Savior. To discover more about covenant security and eighteen other secrets of divine protection, see my book, *The Armor of Light,* Twin Pillars Press, Paradise, CA, 2020. A separately published Study Guide is also available. Books are available from https://michaelchristian.us, Amazon, Barnes & Noble, and fine independent bookstores worldwide.

Though God granted humanity free will, chaos doesn't reign. He does! Amazingly, His divine purposes on earth are still being accomplished without Him limiting man's free will. He "works all things according to the counsel of His will." (Eph. 1:11) Christ will "reign till He has put all enemies under His feet." (1 Cor. 15:25, 24–28) There is a coming judgment in which every person will give an account of their deeds before God. However, the sins of everyone who receives Jesus as their Savior are already forgiven. They will be spared in the judgment and inherit eternal life in heaven with God. (Rev. 20: 11–15, John 5:24, Rom. 5:9)

How Did Evil Come into the Earth?

As the Creator, God is one hundred per cent good and separate from evil. (Rev. 21:27, 2 Cor. 6:14–17) Everything He created was "very good." (Gen. 1:31) Evil was not present in the original creation nor was death. Evil and death entered the world *after* the serpent smooth-talked Adam and Eve into desiring the knowledge of good *and evil.* (Gen. 2:16, 3:1–6, Rom. 5:12) They had the knowledge of good because they knew God and His creation. But the serpent convinced them to seek the knowledge of evil, so they could be wise like God. (They were innocent and had no clue what evil was.)

Because God is all good, only someone who was evil could instruct Adam and Eve in the knowledge of evil.[5] (Matt. 19:17) The serpent gladly stepped into that role. When Adam and Eve ate the forbidden fruit, disobeying God, they joined the devil's rebellion against good and unleashed evil on themselves, their children, and the creation. Because they obeyed the devil, they became his servants and made him their master. (John 8:34, Romans 6:16, John 14:30)

Tragically, Adam and Eve's first lesson in evil came when their older son Cain killed their younger son Abel in a fit of jealous rage. As a result of our first parents being tricked, evil has had permission to influence and afflict the human race ever since.

God never granted evil permission to operate in the earth. He never condoned, caused, or sent it. But our original parents did when they obeyed the serpent and disobeyed God. We, too, have contributed to the evil on earth when we were beguiled by some two-legged serpent into violating the ways of God.

How Do Things Operate Today?

Humanity has a God-given free will to make decisions, but we are influenced by spiritual forces. God influences us to seek Him and do good, and the devil influences us to do evil. Nevertheless, we make the final decisions. The devil can't make you do anything, and God won't force you. The Lord sets before you life and death and counsels you to choose life that you may live. (Deut. 30:15–20)

---

[5] Evil is not a separate creation but a corruption of God's good. It is rebellion against His created order.

But Doesn't God Allow Evil to Refine Our Character?

Not every Christian sees things the way I've outlined here. Many sincere and fine pastors and ministers teach that God micromanages all things, and that He actively sends, assigns, or permits evil circumstances to refine our character. Such teachings can have unintended consequences and turn people away from the Lord.

For instance, I received the following comment on my blog post, "Does God Hire the Spiritual Mafia to Correct His Children?" (https://michaelchristian.us/God's-correction) My article explains why God doesn't use the "great contaminator" (the devil) to purify His children. Here's the comment.

> I was always taught that "God allowed" the most heinous of horrific events to turn them to good. Never bought that but somehow it crept into my soul, making me so afraid of what God might do next to refine me. He shows his love for me, and I love him, but I would never go to church again if you paid me a million after the damage they did to me. So this is a good message!

This person was turned away by the teaching that God controls and uses evil to refine believers. Such a point of view has a big problem: it makes a pure and holy God responsible for all the evil on the planet. While there are different points of view on this profound subject, here's how I look at it.

Why would God, who is love, who sent His Son to bleed and die to redeem us from evil, send more evil across our path to teach us a spiritual lesson? Are the the blood of Christ, the Word of God, the Holy Spirit, and Christ's intercession *insufficient* to teach, correct, and sanctify His people? Is something lacking in the atonement that the Lord needs to hire the spiritual mafia (the devil and his demons) to correct His children? Are we saved and sanctified by grace through faith plus evil?

The author of Hebrews would disagree. He said, "For by *one offering* He has perfected forever those who are being *sanctified*." (Heb. 10:14, 10) The offering of Christ is *sufficient* to sanctify and refine our character forever. The word *sanctify* means to set apart from evil to set apart to God. If God is trying to separate us from evil, why would He send more against us? (Cp. 2 Cor. 6:17–18, 1 John 5:18) Hebrews also says that Christ is *"able to save to the uttermost* [sanctify] *those who come to God through Him, since He always lives to make intercession for them."* (Heb. 7:25)

But if as some say, God employs evil to refine the character of His children, I have another problem. How can I distinguish the hand of God from the hand of the devil? James 4:7 tells me I am to *submit* to God and *resist* the devil. But if evil comes from God as well as the devil, how do I know which evil to submit to and which to resist? How can I live an overcoming life when it's not clear what I am to fight against?

Does God Send Evil That Good May Come?

On the surface, it sounds plausible that God might send us trials to achieve the "good" of making us better and more spiritual. The idea possesses a certain logic, and Romans 8:28 is cited as proof. God does make all things work together for good to those who love God and are called according to His purpose. But the question is, Does He cause the evil so He can turn it to good? I don't think so. However, He does take what the enemy meant to destroy us and turns it around for our good when we pray for strength and endurance during the trial. (Rom. 8:26–27)

The idea of sending evil that good may come adheres to the worldly notion that the end justifies the means. For example, that philosophy says it's okay to steal if I'm doing it for the good end of feeding my family.

But the Lord doesn't believe or practice this idea. Here's why. He set in motion the law of sowing and reaping. That law *contradicts* the idea that the end justifies the means. It states that what a person sows he also reaps.

> Do not be deceived, God is not mocked; *for whatever a man sows, that he will also reap*. For he who sows to his flesh will of the flesh reap corruption, but he who sows to the Spirit will of the Spirit reap everlasting life. —Galatians 6:7–8 (italics added)

The means or methods that are sown (like a seed) determine and shape the end that is reaped (the outcome or harvest). I could choose to lie, cheat, or steal to reach what I see as a good end. However, the corrupt methods I introduce in the process will irreversibly change the good outcome I seek. If I accomplish my end by lying, I destroy the trust of those around me when my lies are found out.

If I use bitter flour to make bread, I end up with bitter bread. If I add a rotten apple to good apples, the pie will taste like a rotten apple. If I perform surgery with a dirty, rusty scalpel, the patient will be infected. No one can employ evil methods and expect good to come. Evil methods contaminate the end result.

The law of sowing and reaping says that the means, methods, and processes used determine the end. You can't use something that is inherently filthy to make something else clean. You don't wash drinking glasses in toilet water.[6] You shouldn't wash white clothes in muddy water if you want them to stay white. Likewise, a holy God will not send the devil, the chief of all unclean spirits and the embodiment of filth and rebellion, to sanctify His people. Why? Evil's rottenness rubs off on those it contacts and makes the end result unclean.

Evil attacks do not come from the Lord. He never assigns or give demons permission to afflict His children to refine their characters. Not only would sending evil

---

[6] I explain this in greater depth in *The Armor of Light*. See Chapter 18, "Is It God or the Devil?" starting on page 134.

spirits corrupt His children, but it would be witchcraft, and God hates witchcraft. (Deut. 18:10) So, why would He practice it?

Should We Expect a Life Without Trials?

If God is not the one sending trouble, should I then expect a life without trials if I have enough faith? No, the world has been full of trouble since Adam and Eve were tricked. Evil is in the world, and we experience it without God doing anything. Jesus said,

> "These things I have spoken to you, that in Me you may have peace. In the world you will have tribulation [trouble]; but be of good cheer, I have overcome the world." —John 16:33

When trials come our way, we can trust the Mighty One to help us through them because He didn't cause them. His Spirit lives in us, and we too can overcome the world. (1 John 5:4)

When Paul returned to the region where he had recently been stoned, he and his team were…

> Strengthening the souls of the disciples, exhorting them to continue in the faith, and saying, "We must through many tribulations enter the kingdom of God." —Acts 14:22

Paul knew tribulations would come from persecution by evil men. But He trusted in God as His deliverer. He said, "And the Lord will deliver me from *every* evil work and preserve me for His heavenly kingdom." (2 Tim. 4:18)

Do we learn lessons when we go through trials? Absolutely! Trials build character. (Rom. 5:3–5) The most accelerated season of character development I've experienced was during the worst of trials. God didn't *send* the trials to make me better, but He strengthened me as I prayed desperate prayers for help and endurance.

You Can Trust That God Is Love

You can trust the Bible that God is love. He did not send, condone, or permit the evil that attacked you. The devil is not in some twisted way on God's payroll, a tool in His tool bag, or His agent on a leash. God is holy and separate from all evil. He has no fellowship with darkness. (Eph. 5:11, 2 Cor. 6:14–18) The "accuser of the brethren" has been permanently cast out of heaven. God has *no* conversations with him about your life nor will He receive accusations from him against you. (John 12:31, Rev. 12:7–10, Rom. 8:33)

The Lord is your answer, your healer, your restorer, and never your problem! Reject the lie that wants you to blame God for what you went through. The enemy was able to attack you because Adam and Eve gave him permission, but in the Lord is your help. Draw near to Him in faith, and He will tow you out of the muddy bog of confusion and restore you to life.

The following prayer has helped many forgive God for what happened to them or their loved ones.

> *Father, I come to You not understanding everything that happened in my life. I expected You to do _____, but it didn't happen. I confess I am confused, discouraged, and even angry. But I place on the altar all my unfulfilled expectations and dreams. I determine to worship You from this day forward without reservation or condition. I receive Your love and restoration. From now on, You will be my God and I will be Your servant, in Jesus' name. Amen.[7]*

The Lord can now take what the enemy intended to destroy you and make all things work together for your good. (Rom. 8:26–28) The harder the enemy hit you, the higher you will rise. God will transmute the lead of your suffering into the gold of His anointing. Keep looking up. Help is on the way! Those who overcome great adversities minister in the power of the Holy Spirit.

And on your last day, the Lord will welcome you into an eternity where there is no more pain, death, sorrow, or crying! (Rev. 21:4)

---

[7] Inspired by the "Prayer for Restoration" in Joan Hunter's book, *Healing the Whole Man Handbook*, Whitaker House, New Kensington, PA, 2006, p. 33.

PART I:

The Word LOVE Throughout The New Testament

But above all these things put on love,
which is the bond of perfection.

—Colossians 3:14

The New Testament Word Sections

Every Greek Word
Translated as any Form of
The Word LOVE

Christ's New Commandment

"A new commandment I give to you, that you love one another; as I have loved you, that you also love one another. By this all will know that you are My disciples, if you have love for one another."

—John 13:34–35

NT WORD 1. AGAPAO

Love Means Action

ἀγαπάω *ag-ap-ah´-o*. Verb. *To love*. (Strong's: G 25)

Many have heard of the *agape* love of God. But what is *agapao*? It is simply the familiar *agape* in a verb form. *Agapao* is *agape love* in action.

Agapao, agape, and agapetos (NT Words 1, 2, and 3) are the word family that represents the highest, purest form of love in the Bible, especially divine love. Actions that demonstrate loyalty and commitment define this kind of love. Godly love values those it loves above its own life. It will deny its own interests and desires to assist its beloved. Jesus said, "Greater love (*agape*) has no one than this, than to lay down one's life for his friends." (John 15:12–13)

Agapao is the *action* of a love that aligns with God's pure standards. (John 13:34, 14:15, Rom. 13:8–10, 1 John 5:3)

To Love as Christ

To *love-agapao* means to love as Jesus Christ loved (John 15:12). It goes beyond loving your friends to loving your enemies and those unlike yourself. When you love with *agapao*, you forgive those who crucify you, bless those who curse you, do good to those who hate you, and pray for those who persecute you. Love gives to meet another's needs without concern for reward or repayment. (Luke 23:34, Matt. 5:43–48, 6:32–35, 14:12–14)

Learning How to Love

Learning to *love-agapao* has two fundamental steps. (1) The first is being born again through faith in Jesus Christ. When you are reconciled to God, you experience the security and joy of being accepted and loved by Him. (2) Then, you discover that God's love is poured out in your heart, and it will flow *through you* in love and grace to others. (Rom. 5:5)

The Love Commands in the Law of Moses

As a child in Sunday School, I memorized the first and second commandments. Jesus spoke of these verses in response to a scribe who asked Him, "Which is the great commandment *in the law*?" (Matthew 22:36, cp. Mark 12:28)

> "And you shall **love** [1. agapao]...the LORD your God with all your heart, with all your soul, with all your mind, and with all your strength." —Mark 12:30

> "You shall **love** [1. agapao]...your neighbor as yourself." —Mark 12:31

As familiar as these commandments have been since childhood, I realize I cannot keep them perfectly, no matter how hard I try. Like the rest of the law, they bring me under conviction of sin and make plain my need of a Savior. The law set such a high standard for love that only Jesus could fulfill it.

Nevertheless, it's helpful to look at what it means to love God with *all* our heart, mind, soul, and strength that we might progress toward that goal. Thankfully, we have received the Holy Spirit, and He encourages us to keep pressing toward the image of perfection.

Loving God with All...

(A) *Your heart* means giving God first place and top priority in your life. It is seeking first His kingdom and righteousness. (Matt. 6:33, cp. 6:24, 19:16–26) This implies having no heart-idols[1] before Him. While we love family and the things we have and do, we can't make them more important than the Lord.

(B) *Your soul* refers to praying to, thanking, praising, adoring, and worshiping God with the totality of your intellect, will, and emotions; surrendering completely to Him with nothing held back and nothing pretended. (Ps. 103:1).

(C) *Your mind* is accepting the Bible as the Word of God, making it your counselor and guide to life. (Ps. 1:1–3, John 6:63, 68) It means meditating daily in the Scriptures that you may renew your mind and think with the mind of Christ. (Josh. 1:8, Rom. 12:2, 1 Cor. 2:16, Phil. 2:5, Col. 3:16)

(D) *Your strength* means doing your utmost in everything, "as to the Lord." It suggests striving for excellence and putting forth a one hundred percent effort, vigorously pursuing those things God commands and commends (Col. 3:23).

As much as we may cherish keeping this ideal, it is impossible to love God with *all* our heart, soul, mind, and strength, no matter how hard we try. In real life in the United States, we turn to family and business, pleasures and pastimes, hobbies and entertainment, rather than giving our full attention to God. We hold onto heart idols we only partially recognize and never dethrone completely. We indulge our flesh rather than living in godly self-discipline with all our strength. We open our minds to thoughts that are not worthy of a child of God. We live with fear, anger, worry, anxiety, lust, greed, bitterness, and discouragement, and then sigh because we're not living fully for God. We fail to love God according to the standard of the law.

---

[1] A heart-idol sits on the throne of our heart. It is anything we love or worship more than God. It can be self, pride, career, money, ambition, power, possessions, pleasure, etc.

Loving My Neighbor

We don't do much better with the second commandment of the law. Neighbor love ministers to whoever around us is in need, no matter their nationality or religious and ethnic background. (Luke 10:25–37, Rom. 13:8–10) It keeps the Golden Rule, doing unto others as we *wish* they would do unto us. (Luke 6:31) But too often, we ignore the needs of our neighbor when it is inconvenient to help or interferes with our plans.

It's Impossible to Keep the Love Commands

What made the first commandment impossible to keep was the little word "all." It demanded we love God with one hundred per cent of our heart, soul, mind, and strength. It left no room for half-hearted actions.

If we moved to a monastery, convent, or a cave and did nothing but pray, read the Bible, and worship all day, we could not keep this commandment perfectly. Something would always interrupt and interfere with our perfect devotion.

Under the law's commands, we are caught between two ideals: loving God with all our heart and loving our neighbor as ourselves. When we pursue one, we neglect the other. It's like coming to a fork in the road, and God commands us to go down both paths because they are right and good.

So, how are we to express our love, loyalty, and commitment to the Lord and to people? Do we bounce between devotion and service? Or, do we pick one path and do our best to travel it?

A New Commandment for a New Covenant

When Jesus died on the cross, He delivered us from the dilemma imposed by the Old Covenant law. He established a *New Covenant* with a *New Commandment* that fulfills the love commands of the law.

At the Last Supper, our Savior made it crystal clear that He was laying down His life to establish the *New Covenant* in His blood. He purposefully coupled that New Covenant with a *New Commandment*. The verse below is the only place in the New Testament that Jesus issued what He called a *"new commandment."* That should make us jump to attention. In John 15:12, He called it *"My commandment."*

> "A *new commandment* I give to you, that you **love [1. agapao]**…one another; as I have **loved [1. agapao]**…you, that you also **love [1. agapao]**…one another. By this all will know that you are My disciples, if you have **love [2. agape]** for one another." —John 13:34–35 (italics added)

Under the New Covenant, we show our devotion to God by loving our brothers and sisters in Christ. We no longer need to isolate ourselves and focus exclusively on God. We can love God and people at the same time. We don't give up our devotional time, and we don't neglect people.

Jesus modeled how to do this. He prayed early in the morning and ministered to people the rest of the day.

If the disciples didn't quite get the message about the uniqueness of the new commandment, He confirmed it later the same evening.

"This is *My commandment,* that you **love [1. agapao]**...one another as I have **loved [1. agapao]**...you." —John 15:12

"These things I *command* you, that you **love [1. agapao]**...one another." —John 15:17

The New Commandment Is More Than the Second Commandment

I assumed (uncritically) for years that the new commandment was simply a restatement of the second commandment. To me, "love your neighbor" sounded very close to "love one another." But Jesus was *not repeating* the second commandment of the law when He addressed the disciples at the Last Supper. He issued an altogether new commandment.

Loving your neighbor *as yourself* was the standard set by the second commandment under the law of Moses. But the new commandment commands us to love one another *more* than ourselves. We are to love *as Christ loved us—and He gave His life for us while we were His enemies. (*Rom. 5:8–10) That is radical love! (John 15:13)

In the Sermon on the Mount, Jesus clarified the difference between the law's second commandment and Christ's new commandment.

"You have heard that it was said, 'You shall **love [1. agapao]**...your neighbor and hate your enemy.' But I say to you, **love [1. agapao]**...your enemies, bless those who curse you, do good to those who hate you, and pray for those who spitefully use you and persecute you." —Matthew 5:43-44

Keeping the second commandment required generous *human* love, loving others as we love ourselves. But loving those who offend and harm us goes beyond human love. It requires a reservoir of *divine love* in the heart to draw from. This amazing resource comes to those who are born again. When we are reconciled to God, who is love, we have access to love's fountain of living waters springing up in our hearts. (Romans 5:5)

According to Jesus, the proof of Christian discipleship is *Christlike love* for the brethren. (1 John 3:16)

Love Revolution

Though I had read the Bible for years and hand copied the love Scriptures, I missed something. I assumed like millions of others that the love commands of the law were the greatest commandments in the Bible, but they aren't. They are the greatest of the

Old Covenant. They are instructive and life-changing, even today, and we don't ignore or abandon them.

But we live under the New Covenant, not the Old. The supreme commandment for the Church is Jesus' New Commandment. We are to love one another as He loved us.

I needed help to understand these things, and I encourage you to take the same wonderful journey I did to rediscover the lost command of Jesus. My eyes were opened by an exceptional book called *Love Revolution* by Pastor Gaylord Enns.[2]

Pastor Enns had served Christ for decades in faithful, fruitful, pastoral service. In his book, he shares through an amazing personal story how the Holy Spirit gently opened his eyes to the significance of Christ's new commandment. His book is well-written and researched, theologically sound, and easy to understand.

Pastor Enns discovered something surprising in his research. The apostles who wrote the Bible's gospels and epistles emphasized Christ's love message. But after the first few centuries of Christianity, Christ's new commandment began to be ignored in sermons, theological writings, creeds, and confessions. Pastor Enns wrote:

> Thus, after many months of research, I came to the sad conclusion that I was not alone in my oversight of Jesus' Command. By and large, love has remained only a *subset* of Christian truth and teaching. It has not been given priority as a *core commandment* of authentic Christianity.[3]

It's a huge omission to ignore Jesus's most unique and distinct "commandment." Most Christians know the verse, "God is love," but do we know what it means to love as Christ loved us? Should we not return to an emphasis of the "first love" He commanded? (Cp. Rev. 2:4)

According to Paul, the hallmark of Christian discipleship is not charismatic gifts, mountain-moving faith, perfect doctrine, or benevolence to the poor, as important as those things are, but *Christlike love* for the brethren. (1 Cor. 13:1–3, 13, see also 1 John 3:16, 23)

I encourage you to get a copy of *Love Revolution*. It should be required reading for all disciples, pastors, and leaders.

Love Is a Decision

When you accepted Christ, God re-created your spirit, the part of you that communes with God. (2 Cor. 5:17, Eph. 4:24) He replaced your dead spirit with a new and living one. Jesus called this being born again. Your born-again spirit is the product of God's skilled workmanship and cannot be improved upon. (Eph. 2:10) Though your

---

[2] Gaylord Enns, *Love Revolution*, (Chico, CA: Love Revolution Press, 2022).
[3] *Love Revolution*, p. 120.

spirit is perfect, you still have to work on your soul (mind, will, and emotions) and controlling your bodily appetites.

While re-creating you, God took away your old stony heart and gave you a new and tender one. He put His Spirit within you. He poured out His love in your heart and placed the fruit of the Spirit in your spirit. (Ezek. 36:26, Rom. 5:5, Gal. 5:22–23) If you are born again, you have God's love in you now.

As a born-again Christian, you *have* the ability to be patient and kind. You can endure the gnawing pain of frustration without lashing out. You can forgive those who have done you wrong. Your soul may harbor carnal feelings and reasons why you don't want to forgive, but if you live out of your spirit, you can. The Holy Spirit in your spirit inspires your soul to live up to a Christlike standard. But your mind requires renewing in the Word to align with what God put in your spirit. (Rom. 12:2)

Loving-agapao is a decision of the will in obedience to the Word, not always a spontaneous emotion. (Cp. Matt. 5:44) Love says, "I *choose* to love you." Once you make the *decision* to love, you will have joy as God works within you "both to will and to do for His good pleasure." (Phil. 2:13) The *decision* to love unconditionally is like the engine of the train. It pulls the load. *Feelings* are the caboose; they come along afterward.

In summary, *agapao* is the *action* of love that springs from a transformed character and the new and Christlike heart. (Ezek. 36:26, Heb. 8:10, 1 Tim. 1:5)

Choosing to love with divine love often runs contrary to human nature, so it's not always easy. It can be more like work. This *labor* of love assigns the duty according to the Word. Then, your spirit and (renewed) mind must school your flesh and emotions to obedience. (1 Thess. 1:3)

Contrasting Human and Divine Love

Agapao can be distinguished from *phileo* (Word 14), the more common, classical Greek verb for love. *Phileo*, in most cases, refers to natural human love, a more or less spontaneous emotion based on feelings, common interests, and mutual response. But *agapao* signifies *an unconditional love that chooses to love regardless of the response it receives! Agapao* is self-sacrificing, willing to lay down its life for its friends.

One remarkable conversation in the Bible pivoted on the meanings of these two words, *agapao* and *phileo*. After His resurrection, Jesus asked Peter, "Simon, son of Jonah, do you *love [1. agapao]* Me more than these?" Or, "Simon, do you love Me with the kind of love that would give its life for Me?" (John 21:15)

On the eve of Christ's crucifixion, Peter had denied the Lord three times after insisting that he would not. He knew he could not answer with *agapao*, the highest kind of love. So, he replied, "Yes, Lord; You know that I *love [14. phileo]* You." Or,

"Lord, you know that I love You with human love and affection." Jesus said, "Feed My lambs!"

Jesus asked the question a second time, and Peter responded the same way. Jesus answered, "Tend My sheep!" (John 21:16)

But the third time, Jesus rephrased the question by changing the word for love. "Simon, son of Jonah, do you *love [14. phileo]* Me?" "Simon, do you love me with human affection? Do you love me with the warmth of human affection that should stand up for its friends?"

Peter was grieved because Jesus asked, "Do you *love [14. phileo]* me with human affection?" He said, "Lord, You know all things; You know that I *love [14. phileo]* You with human affection!" Jesus answered, "Feed My sheep!" (John 21:17)

For each denial, Peter had to reaffirm his love for Jesus. Then the Lord prophesied that when Peter was old, he would lay down his life as Jesus' faithful witness. Tradition tells us that Peter was crucified upside down in Rome.

Does Your Love Show Grace?

When I first copied the passage below, a hand reached out of the pages of the Bible and slapped me gently on the cheek, figuratively speaking.

> "But if you **love [1. agapao]**...those who **love [1. agapao]**...you, what *credit* is that to you? For even sinners **love [1. agapao]** those who **love [1. agapao]** them. And if you do good to those who do good to you, what *credit* is that to you? For even sinners do the same. And if you lend to those from whom you hope to receive back, what *credit* is that to you? For even sinners lend to sinners to receive as much back." —Luke 6:32–34

The King James Version, from which I originally copied, reads like this in verse 32: "For if ye love them which love you, what *thank* have ye? For sinners also love those that love them." The part that got my attention (more than the old form "ye") was this phrase, "what *thank* have ye?" What "thank?" What does that mean? (The New King James Version and other modern versions translate the phrase as "what *credit* is that to you.")

I looked up the word "thank" in the original Greek language. It was translated from *charis,* the Greek word usually translated *grace.* If we substitute the word grace for thank in the passage, the phrase would read, "what *grace* have ye?" (as it is translated in the Young's Literal Translation). The Holy Spirit began to speak to my heart.

What grace do we have if we only love those who love us? What grace do we exhibit or show? As believers in Jesus, we appreciate receiving the unmerited grace of God, which forgives our sins and brings us into right standing with Him. But Jesus expects us to *show grace* to others. Loving those who love you doesn't take much grace. Sinners can do that because it is normal human love.

But it takes grace to love those who do not love you. Imagine that you have done wrong to someone. If you humble yourself, go to them, and repent, it's a personal relief when they forgive you. The relationship is usually restored. But are we willing to show Christlike grace and forgiveness to those who have done us wrong? What grace do *we* show?

Loving those who have hurt or harmed you is not in the realm of natural love. As humans born with a fallen nature, we may be inclined to retaliation and revenge. So, it requires the *agapao/agape* love of God, which is full of grace, to love and forgive those who have offended us. Are you feeling the burn on your cheek like I did?

When we do good only to those who do good to us, we are not showing any grace. If the flow of grace stops with us and doesn't go any further, we frustrate the grace of God. God gives us grace, and He wants us to show the same grace to others. They, in turn, are to show grace to still others. We quench the flow of the Spirit when we shut up our hearts and refuse to extend the same grace to others that we have freely received from God.

Jesus told a parable of a man who owed a great sum of money to the king. The king demanded payment. When the man begged for mercy, the king graciously forgave his debt. But then the man went to collect a very small sum owed him by a fellow servant. That man asked for mercy and time to repay, but the first man threw his fellow into the debtor's prison. This angered the king, who turned the unforgiving man over for punishment until his debt was paid. (Matthew 18:21–35)

The Lord not only desires to get grace to us but to get grace through us. Someone explained the grace-filled love like this: "If I decide to forgive you *before* you get ugly with me, then we don't have a problem."

God's Love Goes Beyond Human Love

Here is Jesus' conclusion:

> "But **love** [1. agapao]…your enemies, do good, and lend, hoping for nothing in return; and your reward will be great, and you will be sons of the Most High. For He is kind to the unthankful and evil. Therefore be merciful, just as your Father also is merciful." —Luke 6:35–36

The sons of the Most High act differently than the people of the world. Their love contains the grace that comes from being loved by God. They don't just love those who love them but their enemies as well. They don't just do good to those who do good to them but to those who hate them. They don't just lend to those who will probably repay them but to others as well.

Jesus explained that the born-again sons of the Most High become like God, who is kind to the unthankful and evil. Therefore He said, "Be merciful, just as your Father also is merciful."

Loving One's Enemies

At the core of Christlike love is the ability to love one's enemies by grace.

"But I say to you, **love** [**1. agapao**]…your enemies, bless those who curse you, do good to those who hate you, and pray for those who spitefully use you and persecute you." —Matthew 5:44

When I first copied these verses as a young Christian, I thought this was impossible. But Jesus provides three keys in this passage to loving your enemies:

- *"Bless" those who curse you:* Loving your enemies begins with *speaking well* of them. When you speak evil of someone, you curse them. When you speak well of them, you bless them. We have to stop speaking evil of the people who curse us or have done us wrong. Instead, say something good about them. Don't keep nursing and rehearsing what they did to you. When you feel the urge to tell someone about it, zip it! Keep your mouth shut. Discipline yourself to break the escalating spiral of evil for evil and railing for railing. (1 Peter 3:9) A soft answer turns away anger. (Prov. 15:1) Say something nice or nothing at all. Don't speak to them as they do to you. They may curse, but you bless. *Don't let other people's conduct determine your own.*

- *"Do good" to those who hate you:* Loving your enemies continues with a positive action. It's hard for someone to hate you if you do something good for them. Look for an opportunity to show kindness to those who hate you. You will have to tear down any stronghold of hate and bitterness in your own heart before you can do this. Set yourself free. Let it go! Do good!

- *"Pray" for those who spitefully use you and persecute you:* Finally, pray for your enemies. Jesus prayed from the cross that God would forgive those who condemned Him to death. He kept his heart clean by forgiveness. His Spirit lives in you, so you can forgive as He did. As you pray for those who did you wrong, God's Spirit may give you insight into their lives and stir sympathy for why they are the way they are. You may end up pitying your enemy because they are ensnared by evil.

Under the Old Covenant, God called Israel to conquer the promised land through military might. Under the New Covenant, believers conquer with the greatest force of all—*love in action*—to transform enemies into friends.

Love disarms the hate in others. You are "more than a conqueror" when you walk in the love of God. (Rom. 8:37) A worldly conqueror destroys and takes prisoners, but

God's love *liberates* those in bondage to hate, sin, fear, the world, the flesh, and the devil.

Contrasting the Four Greek Words for Love

The Greek language has three main words for love and a fourth that describes love within the family unit. Interestingly, each main word expresses a love that originates within one of the three parts of man: spirit, soul, and body. (1 Thess. 5:23) *Agape* love flows from the born-again spirit, *philia* love from the soul, and *eros* love from the body.

Eros

Eros refers to a physical attraction that craves bodily fulfillment. It is a self-centered kind of love that values its pleasure above that of the other person. *Eros* is a manipulator and a taker, seeking intoxication with its own desires. It gives little and takes all. This is the "soap opera" kind of love, lustful and passionate, but never lasting because it takes advantage of and uses people. The word is not found in the New Testament.

Eros possesses and controls the object of its love to satisfy its own urges. People motivated by *eros* use other people to meet their physical needs without a genuine concern for the other's spiritual, emotional, or physical well-being. This kind of attraction looks for chemistry over compatibility. True love is not blind, but *eros* is.

Many people, unfortunately, confuse *eros* (lust) with love. *Eros* demands, "I have needs." This is the cry of a person whose thoughts are dominated by their physical senses (flesh). But in Christ, our physical bodies do not dictate our thoughts and actions. Here's why. The real "you" is not your body but your born-again spirit. Christ's Spirit living in your spirit helps you crucify the flesh with its passions and desires and bring it into subjection to your spirit. (Gal. 5:24, 1 Cor. 9:27) If people can train a horse, you can bring discipline and self-control to your body.

Jesus gives you the ability to possess the vessel of your body in sanctification (holiness) and honor, not in the passion of lust. (1 Thess. 4:3–5) Sexual affection becomes beautiful and fulfilling when it is expressed within a committed, covenant marriage.

Agape love (unlike *eros*) is willing to sacrifice its physical (sexual) desires for the highest good of the other, protecting their purity. (John 15:13) *Agape love* won't lead another into the bondage of a self-centered, self-indulgent, uncommitted (*erotic*) relationship.

Phileo/philia

Phileo (and its noun form *philia*) is *natural human love* based in the soul (the mind, will, and emotions). This is the love of agreement and harmony based on shared affection and common interests. We love the same sports teams, the same movies, and want the same things in life. We love each other because what we have in common is stronger than what might divide us.

Typical human love is reciprocal, or *50/50*. It expects its loving actions to be returned. "Treat me right, and I'll treat you right. Scratch my back, and I'll scratch yours. Love me, and I'll love you." Because human love expects equal effort and mutual benefits, *phileo love* keeps an account. It thinks, "I did this for you, so you owe me." In contrast, *agape love* "keeps no record [accounting] of wrongs." (1 Cor. 13:5 NIV)

The weakness of *phileo love* is the impasse that occurs when each party feels the other "owes" them and needs to level up their account. They both end up waiting for the other to initiate love before they respond. In this situation, only *agape love* has the faith and courage to initiate love and bridge the standoff.

Agapao/agape

Agapao (and its noun form *agape*) puts the other's well-being ahead of its own. It is 100/0, a self-initiating, giving kind of love that doesn't wait for the other to love first. It is an unconditional love sourced in God. *Agapao/agape* says, "I choose to love you regardless of how you've been treating me, regardless of your response—even when your account is running a deficit." This is the love of God! When we were *His enemies*, Jesus chose to initiate love and sacrifice Himself for us! (Rom. 5:8)

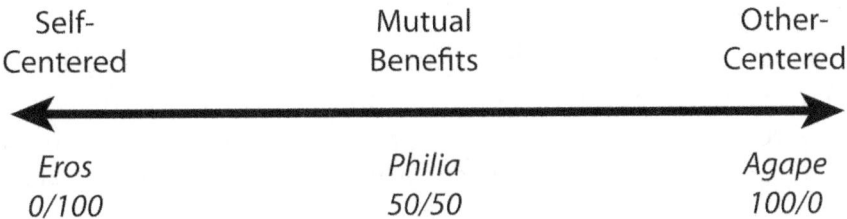

Storge

Storge, a fourth Greek word for love, refers to the warmth of family affection, of parents for children and children for parents. (See Word 4. Astorgos.) *Storge* is human love, such as *phileo*, operating within the family unit. It should be noted that some parents love their children with *agape love*, giving their lives to provide for and raise them as Christ gave Himself for us.

Levels of Love in Marriage

Marital love operates in the same three stages as the three main Greek words. If you want to stay married, you need to get your relationship out of stage one.

(1) The first stage of love is *eros*. *I love you because of how you make me feel*. It's a self-centered love, 0/100. *If you stop making me feel good, I don't love you anymore, and it's all your fault because you no longer do what I want.* This kind of love assumes that its happiness depends on what the other does. But really, my happiness is my choice. It does not rise and fall with the actions of another.

(2) Love's second stage is *phileo*. *If you treat me right, I'll treat you right. You cook dinner; I'll wash the dishes.* This is a 50/50 kind of love. It's fair; it's teamwork; it's shared responsibility. There's equality, reciprocity, and shared benefits. As long as you keep doing things for me, I'll keep doing things for you. Most people consider this the highest kind of love. But if the partners stop making deposits into each other's lives, they run into a problem and no longer "feel" the love they once had. This is remedied by both (or even one) *initiating* loving acts toward the other.

(3) *Agape* is the third and highest level of love. Divine love is 100/0. It sets no preconditions. It initiates love when the relationship is frozen. For example, God, the celestial Husband, remained faithful to Israel when she "divorced" Him to worship idols. Jesus died for our sins, not when we were lovable, but while we were enemies. Mother Teresa cared for lepers who could never repay her except with a whispered, "Thank you."

My neighbor's wife had a stroke and was incapacitated for several years. He faithfully cared for her. His love was one-sided, 100/0. He did all the giving because his wife was incapable of responding. But their story ends well. One day, she miraculously came back to her right mind and could communicate and function again, and they had many more years together.

We become capable of the highest form of love when we find our acceptance and emotional security in the Lord. Our relationship with Him fills us with enough grace to show love for our spouse when they aren't doing anything for us. Divine love is other-centered, desiring what is best for its beloved even at the sacrifice of itself.

In Christ, each spouse becomes the bearer of God's prophetic love message to the other, just like Christ and the Church.

Special Words for Divine Love

The *agapao/agape* word family was rarely used in either classical or common Greek. The words sat like empty vessels waiting to be filled with the sacred meaning of divine love. *Agapao* and *agape* were redefined by their Biblical usage, beginning with their use in translating *'ahab* in the Septuagint, the Greek version of the Old Testament. See OT Word 3. *'Ahab*.

Agapao is also used in a general sense, meaning to love (by choice) a nation, prestige in the eyes of men, mammon, darkness, praise of men, this world, this life, the things of the world, and the wages of unrighteousness.

NT WORD 1. AGAPAO

≔ TRANSLATION TALLY

beloved	7	time(s)	See *You and God*	
love	76	"	" " "	
loved	40	"	" " "	
loves	19	"	" " "	

🖎 YOU AND GOD

Matthew
  5:43, 44, 46 (43–48)
  6:24 (19–25)
  19:19 (16–22)
  22:37, 39 (34–40)
Mark
  10:21 (17–23)
  12:30, 31, 33 (28–34)
Luke
  6:27, 32, 35 (27–36)
  7:5 (2–5)
  7:42, 47 (39–48)
  10:27 (25–29)
  11:43 (42–44)
  16:13 (10–15)
John
  3:16, 19 (14–21)
  3:35 (31–36)
  8:42 (39–43)
  10:17 (14–18)
  11:5 (3–7)
  12:43 (37–43)
  13:1 (1–5)
  13:23 (21–26)
  13:34 (31–35)
  14:15, 21, 23, 24, 28, 31 (15–31)
  15:9, 12 (9–12)
  15:17 (16–19)
  17:23, 24, 26 (22–26)
  19:26 (25–27)
  21:7 (4–8)
  21:15, 16 (13–17)
  21:21 (19–22)
Romans
  8:28, 37 (26–39)
  9:13 (8–13)
  9:25 (21–26)
  13:8, 9 (8–10)
1 Corinthians
  2:9 (6–10)
  8:3 (1–4)
2 Corinthians
  9:7 (6–9)
  11:11 (7–13)
  12:15 (13–17)
Galatians
  2:20 (19–21)
  5:14 (13–18)
Ephesians
  1:6 (3–7)
  2:4 (4–9)
  5:2 (4:30–5:2)
  5:25, 28, 33 (22–33)
  6:24 (21–24)
Colossians
  3:12 (8–14)
  3:19 (18–22)
1 Thessalonians
  1:4 (2–4)
  4:9 (7–10)
2 Thessalonians
  2:13, 16 (13–17)
2 Timothy
  4:8, 10 (5–11)
Hebrews
  1:9 (4–9)
  12:6 (3–7)
James
  1:12 (12–16)
  2:5, 8 (1–9)
1 Peter
  1:8 (5–9)
  1:22 (18–23)
  2:17 (13–17)
  3:10 (10–12)
2 Peter
  2:15 (14–17)
1 John
  2:10 (7–11)
  2:15 (15–17)
  3:10, 11, 14, 18, 23 (10–24)
  4:7, 8, 10, 11, 12 (7–13)
  4:19, 20, 21, 5:1, 2 (4:19–5:4)
2 John
  :1, :5 (1–6)
3 John
  :1 (1–4)
Revelation
  1:5 (4–6)
  3:9 (7–11)
  12:11 (10–12)
  20:9 (7–10)

NT WORD 2. AGAPE

The Love of God

ἀγάπε *ag-ah´-pay.* From *agapao* (see Word 1. Agapao). Noun. *Love.* Strong's: G 26.

Agape is the *love of God,* the highest form of love spoken of in the Bible. God is love. God's nature is *agape.* (1 John 4:8,16)

Agape is the love of God the Father for Jesus Christ, the person of the Holy Spirit, humankind, and creation.

God is often described in terms of His two kinds of attributes, the *non-shared* and the *shared.* His non-shared attributes characterize God and Him alone. These are His sovereignty, omniscience, omnipresence, omnipotence, and so forth. (2) However, God shares His other attributes with His people, including His love, grace, mercy, goodness, truthfulness, and the other fruit of the Spirit.

God's love is one of His *shared* attributes. When you are born again of God, His love is poured out in your heart. (Romans 5:5) With God's love in your heart, you have the capacity to love with God's love and to love what He loves. He calls you to imitate Him in love.

> Beloved, let us **love** [**1. agapao**] one another, for **love** [**2. agape**] is of God; and everyone who **loves** [**1. agapao**] is born of God and knows God. —1 John 4:7

> Therefore be imitators of God as dear children. And walk in **love** [**2. agape**], as Christ also has **loved** [**1. agapao**] us and given Himself for us, an offering and a sacrifice to God for a sweet-smelling aroma. —Ephesians 5:1–2

God Loves You

God loves *you* with *agape love.* He gave His best, His only begotten Son, to die on the cross so that you may have a direct, personal relationship with Him. God wants you to see, know, taste, and experience His love for you as the unique person you are. (John 3:16)

When humanity was living in darkness, God made a way for you to enter His presence. (John 14:6) Have you invited God's best into your heart and life? *Jesus* is the door of access to the Father-love of God! (John 10:7–10, 14:6, Eph. 2:17–18) See *"Experiencing God's Love for the First Time,"* page 13.

Contrary to public opinion, becoming a Christian is not about obeying a set of rules to earn God's favor. It's about getting to know God through faith in Jesus. In Christ, you come to realize that God loves you despite your warts, freckles, and past mistakes. He discounts your past, values your present, and has prepared a glorious future that begins in this life and ends in His big house in heaven.

Love Means Giving

Agape is the divinely-inspired ability to show love by selfless actions, by *giving* of yourself, by *sharing* acceptance, encouragement, prayer, forgiveness, kindness, mercy, courtesy, patience, purity, peace, the Word of God, the Spirit of God, faith, hope, fairness, firmness, persistence, thoughtfulness, talents, time, treasure, labor, gifts, goods—or, in short, *giving* of your life and substance. The reward of *agape love* is the inward joy of loving and giving rather than receiving in return. (Acts 20:35)

Love Is Unconditional

Agape results from *a personal, one-sided decision to love unconditionally like the sun.* Think about it: the sun sheds its encouraging, life-giving radiance on the evil and the good, *regardless of their response!* (Matt. 5:45, 44) The sun receives complaints every day: some say it's too hot, and others say it's not hot enough. Love determines to shine, no matter how its light and warmth are received. Love adopts a lifestyle of giving, *choosing* to initiate love rather than waiting to be its beneficiary.

Loving unconditionally requires a source of love to sustain and refill you. You find it in God's never-failing love for you that refreshes your spirit.

Love Springs from a New Nature

Agape is more than a transitory emotion. It arises from your *new nature* in Christ. When God re-created your spirit, you became *a partaker of His divine nature, which includes His love.* (2 Peter 1:4, Eph. 4:24)

Human emotions come out of the soul, but God's love issues from your spirit, from the *new creation* inside you. God designed your born-again spirit to pour forth the love of God like an artesian spring of living water. (John 4:14, 7:38, Ezek. 36:25–27)

Once you have God's love in your spirit, you love what He loves. (2 Cor. 5:17, Rom. 5:5) He loves all people—even the unruly ones, the ones that drive you up the wall! He loves the creation that He lovingly made, including reptiles, snakes, and bugs. When you have the Creator's love in your heart, you love the creatures He created even if you can't imagine why He made some of them.

Love Requires Crucifixion of Self

Agape becomes possible as we crucify our selfish desires by the indwelling power of the Holy Spirit. (Rom. 8:13, Gal. 5:24) God's love begins to flow when our motives change from the pursuit of self-interest to pleasing God and serving others. Love puts God's good pleasure above our own, and we find our will in His.

Jesus Demonstrated Agape-Love on the Cross

Jesus demonstrated *agape love* through His obedient death on the cross, giving His all for the redemption and healing of humanity. He offered His sinless *spiritual life* to replace and burn away the spiritual death in us. (Matt. 20:28, Lev. 17:11)

The blood of Jesus was saturated with *agape love*. The envy and malice in those who crucified Him could not quench His love. While in agony, He prayed for their forgiveness, "Father, forgive them, for they do not know what they do." (Luke 23:34)

So irresistible is the love of Jesus that *no one* who comes to Him is rejected. None is considered too dirty to be bathed, forgiven, and healed by the gracious flow of this heavenly fountain. Jesus welcomes all who believe in Him into His Father's house and the family of God. (John 6:37)

Christ's *agape* births *agape* in those who believe in Him. (1 John 4:7, 19)

Love Is Full of Grace

Agape is *a grace-filled love* that loves the unlovely and the unworthy. God loves us through no merit of our own because His nature is love. Even when we were His enemies, He gave Himself for us. (Rom. 5:8–10) Experiencing His grace gives us the ability to love by grace, as He does.

Love Is the Fruit of the Spirit

Your ability to love is the fruit of your born-again spirit filled with God's Spirit. (Gal. 5:22–23, Phil. 1:9–11) When you walk in the fruit of the Spirit, you reveal outwardly what you are inwardly—a new creation conformed to the image of Christ. (2 Cor. 5:17, Rom. 8:29)

The Love Chapter

We find the best description of *agape love* in 1 Corinthians 13, the Bible's "Love Chapter." Someone suggested substituting "Jesus" in place of the word "love" in verses 4–8. Does it fit? Now, substitute your name in place of the word "love." How does it compare? What do you need to work on?

The Love Chapter deserves further explanation, and you'll find more on page 67. Many see a *second* love chapter in Romans 12:9–21. There, Paul outlines how to *apply* the grace He describes so eloquently in Romans 1–11. The words, "Let love be without hypocrisy," function like a subtitle for what follows.

Love Shines During Trials

Agape's characteristics are selflessness, patience, and cheerful love even under the darkest of circumstances. Trials test the strength of our love walk. Those who keep their hearts cleansed by quick repentance and forgiveness can maintain their love in challenging situations. (Cp. Matt. 24:12, Prov. 4:23)

Love Springs from Strength

Agape is a learned moral duty and a principled love—the sweet, tender fruit of a hardwood tree ingrained with righteousness. (Isa. 61:3) Love is the fruit of self-mastery, like refreshing water springing from the rock of a Christlike character. (Ps. 78:16, 105:41, 1 Cor. 10:4)

Notice the paradoxes of love: *hardwood* trees bear *soft, tender* fruit, and refreshing *water* flows out of the hard *rock*. (Deut. 8:15, Psalm 114:7–8) It takes strength of character to walk in tender love.

Someone said that people will follow a strong, demanding leader to the ends of the earth *if they know that leader loves them.*

Love Is Not a Pushover

Agape love seeks the highest good of the other without overlooking itself. It has the firmness to confront and set boundaries when another chooses a course of action that is less than God's best, prayerfully speaking the truth in love. (Eph. 4:14–15) It has the strength to say "No," and mean it. *Agape love* is the right combination of a tough mind and a tender, compassionate heart.

When Love Grows Cold

In Matthew 24:12, Jesus warned what would happen in the last days: "And because lawlessness will abound, the **love [2. agape]** of many will grow cold." Jesus linked an increase in lawlessness to a diminishing of love. Lawlessness comes from a disregard of God and His fundamental laws of life and love.

But love is the unifying bond that builds community and knits the "social fabric" together. Paul described how it works.

> Owe no one anything except to **love [1. agapao]** one another, for he who **loves {1. agapao]** another has fulfilled the law. For the commandments, "You shall not commit adultery," "You shall not murder," "You shall not steal," "You shall not bear false witness," "You shall not covet," and if there is any other commandment, are all summed up in this saying, namely, "You shall **love [1. agapao]** your neighbor as yourself." **Love [2. agape]** does no harm to a neighbor; therefore **love [2. agape]** is the fulfillment of the law. —Romans 13:8–10

We do not *earn* salvation by keeping the above commandments, but we show our obedience to Christ's Love Command. Jesus' commanded us to "love one another, *as I have loved you."* (John 13:34)

How did Jesus love us? First, He laid down His life for us, dying the death we deserved. Second, He kept the commandments Paul listed because they are laws of love. He committed no adultery, murder, theft, false witness, or covetousness. In obeying Jesus' Love Command, we ought to walk as He walked. (1 John 2:3–6) "Love does no harm to its neighbor; therefore love is the fulfillment of the law."

In a lawless society, there is no respect for parents, authorities, God, or His wisdom, and these simple rules are ignored. Trust is destroyed, and the social fabric that binds people together disintegrates.

Walking in love requires integrity in the five areas of trust outlined by the commandments. Where adultery, murder, theft, false witness, and covetousness abound, trust is broken, and love grows cold. It's difficult to love when we cannot trust.

But when we walk in the love of God, we respect God, look out for the best interests of our neighbors, and keep the commands to do no harm. Obeying the commandments builds the bonds of love and trust and strengthens the "social fabric," our sense of community and solidarity. John wrote:

> By this we know that we **love [1. agapao]** the children of God, when we **love [1. agapao]** God and keep His commandments. For this is the **love [2. agape]** of God, that we keep His commandments. And His commandments are not burdensome. —1 John 5:2–3

The Love of the Truth

Paul warned that there would be so much unrighteous deception in the last days that only those who received "the love [2. agape] of the truth" would be saved." (2 Thess. 2:10) In talking about the last days, Jesus cautioned, "Take heed that no one deceives you." (Matt. 24:4) We must not only know the truth, we must love, cling to, and adhere to the truth with strength of character. God's Word is our only protection from the deception of the last days.

Love Requires Discernment

More than a feeling, genuine love is full of spiritual knowledge and discernment. It approves things that are excellent, living in purity and sincerity without ulterior motives. (Phil. 1:9–10, 1 Peter 1:22) Walking in uprightness of heart is walking in love. (1 John 5:2–3)

Love Stays Close to its Source

Agape love can give and give and not be exhausted because it is sustained through its personal relationship with God. His boundless love is a reservoir of comfort, healing, inspiration, and virtue. He visits and refills those whose reserves are shared and spent, for God rewards *and replenishes* a cheerful giver. (2 Cor. 9:7)

Love Is a Light in the Darkness

People who love walk in God's light. Those who hate walk in darkness. (1 John 1:6–7, 2:8–11, John 8:12) Divine light and glory in a person express themselves as love, never as hatred, strife, and envy. Love is the manifestation or fruit of the light. (Cp. Eph. 5:9, NIV)

Faith Works by Love

Love is the dynamic that makes faith work. "For in Jesus Christ neither circumcision nor uncircumcision avails anything, *but faith working through love.*" (Gal. 5:6) When your faith isn't working, check your love walk. A lack of love hinders faith. What is not motivated by love is nothing. (1 Cor. 13:2) Your faith becomes powerful when you walk in love, and your love increases when you walk in faith.

Love Is a Conqueror

Love is an effective weapon of spiritual warfare. It is mightier than unforgiveness and conquers enemies by turning them into friends. (2 Cor. 10:4) Jesus conquered *our* hearts when we were His enemies by showing us love rather than judgment, and mercy rather than condemnation. (Rom. 5:10) We can love as He loves because His love has been poured into our hearts. (Rom. 5:5)

Love Builds Up

The body of Christ is built up and edified in love. (1 Cor. 8:1–3, Eph. 4:11–16) Strife, division, and discord weaken and destroy it, but love encourages, heals, and unites the body, producing peace and fruitfulness. (Eph. 4:1–3, Matt. 12:25)

The Love of God

The phrase "the love of God" usually means the love *which God possesses, God's* love, *God's* kind and quality of love. (John 5:42, Rom. 5:5, 8:29, etc.) *We* can love as He loves because His love is in us.

Occasionally, "the love of God" refers to our love *for* God. (1 John 5:3) The two are interrelated. God's manifested love for us produces a loving response in our hearts toward Him. (1 John 4:19)

⋮≡ Translation Tally

love	114	time(s)	See *You and God*
love feasts	1	"	Jude :12
love's	1	"	Philemon :9

 You and God

Matthew
  24:12 (9–14)
Luke
  11:42 (42–44)
John
  5:42 (37–43)
  13:35 (33–35)
  15:9,10,13 (9–15)
  17:26 (24–26)
Romans
  5:5, 8 (1–8)
  8:35, 39 (35–39)
  12:9 (9–14)
  13:10 (8–10)
  14:15 (13–17)
  15:30 (29–33)
1 Corinthians
  4:21 (18–21)
  8:1 (1–4)
  13:1, 2, 3, 4, 8, 13,
  14:1 (13:1–14:3)
  16:14 (13–16)
  16:24 (19–24)
2 Corinthians
  2:4, 8 (4–9)
  5:14 (13–15)
  6:6 (3–7)
  8:7, 8 (6–9)
  8:24 (22–24)
  13:11, 14 (9–14)
Galatians
  5:6 (1–6)
  5:13, 22 (13–26)
Ephesians
  1:4 (3–7)
  1:15 (15–20)
  2:4 (4–9)
  3:17, 19 (14–19)
  4:2 (1–6)
  4:15, 16 (13–16)
  5:2 (4:31–5:3)
  6:23 (21–24)
Philippians
  1:9 (8–11)
  1:17 (14–18)
  2:1, 2 (1:27–2:2)
Colossians
  1:4, 8, 13 (3–14)
  2:2 (1–3)
  3:14 (12–15)
1 Thessalonians
  1:3 (2–4)
  3:6, 12 (5–13)
  5:8, 13 (6–14)
2 Thessalonians
  1:3 (2–4)
  2:10 (8–12)
  3:5 (1–5)
1 Timothy
  1:5 (3–7)
  1:14 (12–15)
  2:15 (11–15)
  4:12 (12–16)
  6:11 (8–11)
2 Timothy
  1:7, 13 (6–14)
  2:22 (20–22)
  3:10 (10–12)
Titus
  2:2 (1–5)
Philemon
  :5, :7, :9 (4–13)
Hebrews
  6:10 (7–12)
  10:24 (21–25)
1 Peter
  4:8 (7–11)
  5:14 (12–14)
2 Peter
  1:7 (4–8)
1 John
  2:5 (3–6)
  2:15 (15–17)
  3:1 (1–3)
  3:16, 17 (16–19)
  4:7, 8, 9, 10, 12, 16,
    17, 18,
  5:3 (4:7–5:4)
2 John
  :3, :6 (1–6)
3 John
  :6 (4–8)
Jude
  :2 (1–4)
  :12 (11–13)
  :21 (20–25)
Revelation
  2:4 (2–5)
  2:19 (18–20)

The Love Chapter
1 Corinthians 13

Detailed plans for a new home can be overwhelming if you are not a building professional. When you read the materials list, you wonder what some of the items are. But as the building takes shape, it all makes sense.

The Love Chapter is the blueprint to build you into a person of Christlike love. If you are a new Christian, the description may seem overwhelming at first. But realize, Paul is describing the ideal person walking in perfect love. Learning to love like Jesus is the work of a lifetime, and none of us has arrived. Only He walked the love walk flawlessly. Some aspects of love may be fairly easy for you while others will stretch you beyond your present capacity. As you practice these truths, you'll see the wisdom behind them.

The Love Chapter

The "Love Chapter" of the Bible, 1 Corinthians 13, gives the best description of love in the Bible. It begins with these three verses.

> Though I speak with the tongues of men and of angels, but have not **love [2. agape]**, I have become sounding brass or a clanging cymbal. And though I have the gift of prophecy, and understand all mysteries and all knowledge, and though I have all faith, so that I could remove mountains, but have not **love [2. agape]**, I am nothing. And though I bestow all my goods to feed the poor, and though I give my body to be burned, but have not **love [2. agape]**, it profits me nothing. —1 Corinthians 13:1–3

Religious expressions are hollow-sounding if we have not love. Speaking in tongues, prophesying, preaching, teaching the mysteries of God, plumbing the depths of theology, and exercising mountain-moving faith, if not motivated by love, are nothing. Giving large charitable gifts, ministering to the poor and disenfranchised, and even dying as a martyr, if not done with love, are unprofitable.

Notice, the Holy Spirit touches on every aspect of Christian ministry here—preaching, teaching, charismatic gifts, theology, benevolence, and even martyrdom. What is the point? Whatever we do must be motivated by love.

In the verses that follow, the Love Chapter describes sixteen characteristics of love. It lists eight things love is and eight things love is not. (It often helps our understanding to define what something is not.)

> **Love [2. agape]** suffers long and is kind; **love [2. agape]** does not envy; **love [2. agape]** does not parade itself, is not puffed up; does not behave rudely, does not seek its own, is not provoked, thinks no evil; does not rejoice in iniquity, but rejoices in the truth; bears all things, believes all things, hopes all things, endures all things. **Love [2. agape]** never fails... —1 Corinthians 13:4–8a

Here is the list of what love is and what it is not.

Love Is

- *Patient:* long-suffering, enduring, even-tempered
- *Kind:* humane, sympathetic, helpful
- *Rejoicing in the truth* of Christ rather than the world's hollow lies
- *Bearing up under everything:* being a protective cover for others
- *Believing all things:* believing the best of every person
- *Hoping all things:* even in dark and desperate circumstances
- *Enduring everything:* without weakening
- *Never failing:* not suffering defeat or ruin

Love Is Not

- *Envious:* jealous, wanting what another has, discontent, covetous
- *Boastful:* parading and promoting itself, bragging, condescending
- *Arrogant:* puffed up, proud, inflated, blinded by the smoke of conceit
- *Rude:* defying social and moral standards, being inappropriate, shameful and embarrassing
- *Demanding:* clamoring for or seeking its own desires or way
- *Easily provoked:* quickly stirred up or upset in its emotions, overreacting
- *Keeping mental records of wrongs:* real or imagined
- *Rejoicing when bad things happen* to those it doesn't like

The Fruit of Two Trees

We can view this list as the fruit of two very different trees. The first is the Tree of Divine Love. The second is the Tree of Self-Love. The fruit of the second tree describes fallen human nature.

REJOICES IN TRUTH   BEARS ALL THINGS

KIND   BELIEVES ALL THINGS   HOPES ALL THINGS

PATIENT   LOVE NEVER FAILS   ENDURES ALL THINGS

DIVINE LOVE

The Tree of Divine Love

ARROGANT   RUDE, UNBECOMING

BOASTFUL   DEMANDS ITS OWN WAY   EASILY PROVOKED

ENVIOUS   REJOICES IN INIQUITY   KEEPS RECORDS OF WRONGS

SELF LOVE

The Tree of Self-Love

The fruit of Divine Love is produced by those born again of God *and living transformed lives*. All born-again Christians *can* walk in the love of God, but some don't do so consistently. They have not renewed their minds, still think like the world, and act much as they did before they were saved.

Turning Negatives into Positives

Let's take the negatives of Self-Love and restate them in a positive way.

- Love is not envious but *content*.
- Love is not boastful and arrogant but *humble*.
- Love does not act rudely and out of place but is *courteous and gracious*.
- Love does not demand its own way but *gives preference to others*.
- Love is not touchy and irritable but *refuses to be offended*.
- Love does not keep a record of wrongs but *forgives and forgets*.
- Love does not rejoice when bad things happen to people but *mourns evil*.

The Master List of Love's 16 Characteristics

By combining the eight things love is with the eight positives from above, we create a master list of love's characteristics. Love is…

- *Patient:* long-suffering, enduring, even-tempered, not easily angered
- *Kind:* helpful, sympathetic, humane
- *Content:* peaceful, not envious, jealous, covetous, or discontent
- *Humble:* not boastful, arrogant, or self-promoting
- *Courteous:* acts becomingly, sensitive to its surroundings, not rude or out of place
- *Yielding to other's preferences:* not incessantly demanding its own way
- *Unoffendable:* not touchy, irritable, or easily upset
- *Forgives and forgets:* lets offenses go and refuses to keep a record of them
- *Sorrowful when evil happens,* even to one's enemies

- *Rejoices with others in the truth of Christ*
- *Bears up under anything and everything that comes:* holding up under stress and being a protective cover for others
- *Believes all things:* believing the best of every person
- *Hopes all things:* even in desperate circumstances
- *Endures everything:* without weakening
- *Love never fails:* it never suffers defeat or is ruined

At the end of the chapter, Paul summarizes everything by saying,

"And now abide faith, hope, **love [2. agape]**, these three; *but the greatest of these is **love [2. agape]**.*" —1 Corinthians 13:13

Where Should I Begin?

This list is overwhelming if you are new to walking in love. It certainly was to me. But when I didn't know where to begin, someone gave me an insight. They said, "Focus on the first two items: *love is patient,* and *love is kind.*" Instead of sixteen things, I worked on two. I started practicing patience and kindness.

If you are patient and don't blow up at people in anger, even when they've embarrassed you or are costing you money, they'll believe you're walking in love. If you are kind to everyone you meet, even those with nothing to offer you, people will feel that you are walking in love, because you are. Patience and kindness are two of the strongest indicators of your love. Start with them and the others will begin to fall into place. You can do all things through Christ who strengthens you.

NT WORD 3. AGAPETOS

Messages to His Beloved

ἀγαπητός *ag-ap-ay-tos′*. From *agapao* (Word 1). Adjective. *Beloved*. Strong's: G 27.

Agapetos is the word God chose to express His love for His only begotten Son: "This is My *beloved [3. agapetos]* Son, in whom I am well pleased." (Matt. 3:17) God loves Jesus with sincere love. He admired, respected, and esteemed the pure life Jesus lived on earth in perfect faith, love, and obedience. (Cp. Heb. 1:8–9)

Jesus, the beloved Son, dwelt in the bosom of the Father and knew the Father's heart intimately. (John 1:18) He came to declare His greatest joy, the experience of His Father's love. (John 3:16) He prayed that "the love with which You [the Father] loved Me may be in them, and I in them." (John 17:26) God loves you as He loves Jesus because *you are in Jesus, and He is in you.*

Beloved is also the word of tender affection the apostles used in their letters to the churches. They addressed their readers as *beloved* before bringing a fresh word of comfort, edification, exhortation, or warning. Pay close attention to these verses. The presence of *agapetos* is like a highlight marker emphasizing verses of wisdom meant to be remembered and obeyed. (e.g., Rom. 12:19, Phil. 2:12, 1 Peter 2:11, etc.)

Read each verse containing *agapetos* with care—take heed how you hear. The Holy Spirit uses this heart-tugging word to prompt all hearers to obey these principles out of their love for God.

⋮≡ TRANSLATION TALLY

beloved	59	times	See *You and God*
dear	3	"	Eph 5:1, Col 1:7, 1Th 2:8

✍ YOU AND GOD

Matthew
   3:17 (13–17)
   12:18 (15–21)
   17:5 (1–6)
Mark
   1:11 (9–12)
   9:7 (2–8)
   12:6 (1–12)
Luke
   3:22 (21–22)
   9:35 (28–36)
   20:13 (9–16)
Acts
   15:25 (23–29)
Romans
   1:7 (7–9)

   11:28 (25–29)
   12:19 (17–21)
   16:5, 8, 9, 12 (3–13)
1 Corinthians
   4:14, 17 (14–17)
   10:14 (11–15)
   15:58 (54–58)
2 Corinthians
   7:1 (6:14–7:1)
   12:19 (17–19)
Ephesians
   6:21 (21–24)
Philippians
   2:12 (12–15)
   4:1 (3:20–4:1)

Colossians
   4:7, 9 (7–9)
   4:14 (12–15)
1 Timothy
   6:2 (1–2)
2 Timothy
   1:2 (1–2)
Philemon
   :1, :2 (1–3)
   :16 (15–17)
Hebrews
   6:9 (7–10)
James
   1:16, 19 (12–21)
   2:5 (5–7)

1 Peter
   2:11 (11–12)
   4:12 (12–16)
2 Peter
   1:17 (16–18)
   3:1, 8, 14, 15, 17 (1–18)
1 John
   3:2 (1–3)
   3:21 (18–22)
   4:1, 7, 11 (1–11)
3 John
   :1, :2, :5, :11 (1–14)
Jude
   :3 (3–4)
   :17, 20 (17–21)

NT WORD 4. ASTORGOS

Love Toward Family

ἄστοργος *as´-tor-gos*. From *a-* (a particle of negation) and *storge* (love of kindred). *Without family affection.* Strong's: G 794.

Storge, the root of the subject word, refers to the *natural affection* of parents for children and children for parents. *Astorgos* means the opposite, *without natural affection* or *loveless.*

In the two passages containing *astorgos,* the Word of God paints a dark picture of what happens when humanity puts God out of mind. Paul called them "perilous times." (2 Tim. 3:1) Sin, selfishness, and violence are rampant.

Astorgos is a tragic consequence of this epidemic as sin destroys love within the family unit. It's easy to understand why God opposes ungodliness when we see children's lives damaged by the breakdown of love in the family.

Born-again Christians are partakers of the forgiveness, grace, and love imparted by Jesus. With His help, we can overcome our past personal failures, ignorance, and societal trends to become a loving strength to our family. (2 Tim. 1:7)

Restoration of family love is high on God's agenda. As the family goes, so goes society.

≔ TRANSLATION TALLY

unloving   2   times   See *You and God*

YOU AND GOD

Romans	2 Timothy
1:31 (28–32)	3:3 (1–5)

74 / LOVE THROUGHOUT THE NEW TESTAMENT

NT WORD 5. PHILADELPHIA

Brotherly Love

φιλαδελφία *fil-ad-el-fee´-ah*. From *philadelphos* (Word 6). Noun. *Brotherly love*. Strong's: G 5360.

Philadelphia is the special bond Christians have for each other even when they don't know each other. Those born again of the same Father are brothers and sisters in Christ. They are spiritually united as members of the family of God, regardless of age, gender, culture, race, or denominational persuasions. As the Christian family, we love each other with kindly affection, preferential honor, and spiritual purity.

Paul encourages the church to guard and preserve the unity of the Spirit in the bond of peace. We have one Lord, one faith, one baptism, and one God and Father of all! (Eph. 4:3–6)

Brotherly love keeps the New Commandment:

> "A new commandment I give to you, that you **love [1. agapao]** one another; as I have **loved [1. agapao]** you, that you also **love [1. agapao]** one another. By this all will know that you are My disciples, if you have **love [2. agape]** for one another." —John 13:34–35

We express brotherly love by *agape love* for our brothers and sisters in Christ. Cp. 1 Cor. 12:13, 1 John 2:9–11, 3:11–19, 4:20–5:2 and the verses below.

☰ TRANSLATION TALLY

brotherly kindness	2	time(s)	2 Peter 1:7
brotherly love	3	"	See *You and God*
love of the brethren	1	"	" " "

 YOU AND GOD

Romans	1 Thessalonians	Hebrews	1 Peter
12:10 (9–15)	4:9 (7–10)	13:1 (1–6)	1:22 (18–23)

NT WORD 6. PHILADELPHOS

Brother-Loving

φιλάδελφος *fil-ad´-el-fos*. From *philos* (*friendly, loving*) and *adelphos* (*brother*). Adjective. *Brother-loving*. Strong's: G 5361.

Peter outlines the attitude Christians should have toward their brethren in the Lord. As children of the household of God, we are to walk in unity through the tenderness, humility, and courtesy of love.

He warns us not to return evil for evil like the world. We break that downward spiral of retaliation by speaking love, blessings, and forgiveness to those who revile us or do us evil. Our obedience causes us to inherit a blessing, and our prayers will not be hindered.

TRANSLATION TALLY

love as brothers   1   time   See *You and God*

YOU AND GOD

1 Peter
3:8 (7–12)

NT WORD 7. PHILAGATHOS

A Lover of the Good

φιλάγαθος *fil-ag´-ath-os*. From *philos* (*friendly, loving*) and *agathos* (*good*). Adjective. *Loving what is good*. Strong's: G 5358.

Philagathos means loving what is good, excellent, and worthy, whether of men or things. The word *agathos* describes what is inwardly good and wholesome—good men, good trees, good fruit, good words, good works, the incomparably good God (Matt. 19:17), a good heart, good ground, etc.

Philagathos is a qualification for pastors, elders, and overseers. (See Titus 1:8 and 1 Tim. 3:1–7) They must be *lovers of goodness:* (1) loving to do good, (2) setting a high moral standard for themselves as an example to others; (3) overcoming evil with good (Compare Rom. 12:21, Phil. 4:8); and (4) loving what is good. *Philagathos* pastors see the good in everyone, uncover it, draw it out, nurture it, and help it grow strong through the Word.

A word of opposite force, *aphilagathos*, appears in 2 Timothy 3:3 and is translated as "despisers of good." Sadly, that is a characteristic of people in the last days.

≔ TRANSLATION TALLY

a lover of what is good   1   time   See *You and God*

 YOU AND GOD

Titus
 1:8 (5–9)

NT WORD 8. PHILANDROS

Husband-Loving

φίλανδρος *fil'-an-dros*. From *philos* (*friendly, loving*) and *aner* (*man, husband*). *Husband-loving*. Strong's: G 5362.

The Holy Spirit directs mature Christian ladies to teach younger Christian ladies to love their husbands and their children (see Word 16. Philoteknos). The example of older, godly women encourages younger women to put off worldly attitudes and lifestyles and to cultivate Christian values and priorities. Women are to minister to their husbands and families with love and care, becoming models of virtue and levelheadedness.

The faithful, believing wife who sincerely loves, respects, encourages, and prays for her husband strengthens him. Her presence makes him more valuable to the kingdom of God. (Cp. Prov. 18:22) She is to him a lesson in goodness, often in mercy, a sensible confidante, and a helper suitable for him. (Cp. Prov. 31:10–31)

If her husband cares for her as Christ loves the church, together they become living witnesses of the power and blessing of Christian marriage. (Eph. 5:21–33)

Philandros was often inscribed on gravestones in ancient times as a husband's touching tribute to his wife's loving devotion.

TRANSLATION TALLY

love their husbands   1   time   See *You and God*

 YOU AND GOD

Titus
  2:4 (1–5)

NT WORD 9. PHILANTHROPIA

Love for Humanity

φιλανθρωπία *fil-an-thro-pee´-ah*. From *philanthropos*, a compound of *philos* (*friendly, loving*) and *anthropos* (*man*). Noun. *Love for humanity, kindliness.* Strong's: G 5363.

Philanthropia is used twice in the New Testament. The first use records the unusual kindness of the Maltese islanders to a shipful of strangers shipwrecked on their shores (Acts 28:1–10). The second instance applies to the loving act of God in sending a lifeboat, the ark Jesus Christ, to a humanity shipwrecked and perishing in the raging waters of sin, rebellion, and ignorance (Titus 3:4).

The phrase "kindness (*chrestotes*) and love toward man (*philanthropia*)" found in Titus 3:4 was used in the ancient world in praise of gods and secular rulers. Paul applies it to the One who truly merits the description. God the Father's unilateral gift of Jesus Christ to this world is *the pattern* of genuine lovingkindness, of true "philanthropy." (John 3:16)

God was willing to send His only begotten Son to rescue, regenerate, and make us joint heirs with Him. In light of Jesus' sacrifice, how can we give anything less than our whole lives in thankful service to Him who commuted our death sentences by His mercy?

≔ TRANSLATION TALLY

kindness	1	time	Acts 28:2
love...toward man	1	"	See *You and God*

 YOU AND GOD

Titus
   3:4 (3–7)

LOVE THROUGHOUT THE NEW TESTAMENT / 79

NT WORD 10. PHILARGURIA

Love of Money

φιλαργυρία *fil-ar-goo-ree´-ah*. From *philarguros* (Word 11). Noun. *Love of money*. Strong's: G 5365.

Well-translated "love of money," *philarguria* speaks of *greed*, an excessive desire for riches and wealth that results in *miserliness*.

The Bible declares, "For the *love of money [philarguria]*...is *a* root of all kinds of evil." This oft-quoted Scripture outlines the perils of allowing a root of money love to grow in your heart. They include falling into "temptation and a snare," "many foolish and harmful lusts," sinking into "destruction and perdition," straying "from the faith," and being "pierced...through with many sorrows." (See 1 Tim. 6:10 and Prov. 28:20)

The Bible does not define possessing money as a root of all evil, but the "love of money." (The love of money is one form of *covetousness,* which is *the* root of all evil. See Col. 3:5, Eph. 5:5, Deut. 20:3)

Rich and poor alike are endangered by money love when it becomes a heart idol or a life goal. Sometimes, poor people who lack money are trapped by the love of it. But others who have little give cheerfully for the love of Christ. (2 Cor. 8:1–5) Some rich people love, trust, and hoard money, and others use their money as a tool for the kingdom of God.

A root of money love can be plucked out of everyone's heart, rich or poor, by learning and living what Jesus taught in Matthew 6:19–34, 13:22, Mark 10:17–31, and Luke 6:38. With the Holy Spirit's help, we overcome the love of money as He puts His laws in our minds and writes them on our hearts. (Heb. 8:10) What is impossible with man is possible with the Holy Spirit.

Trusting in God rather than riches, contentment with what we have (Phil. 4:11, 1 Tim. 6:6, Heb. 13:5), and consistent tithing and giving clear the heart of the briar patch of money love. (2 Cor. 9:5–11, Prov. 3:9–10) Handling money according to God's Word prepares us to receive bountifully from Him "who gives us richly all things to enjoy." (1 Tim. 6:17–19)

Philarguria can be distinguished from the broader term for "covetousness," *pleonexia*, which means *a continual thirst to have more*. (Luke 12:15, Col. 3:5, etc.)

:≣ Translation Tally

love of money   1   time   See *You and God*

 You and God

1 Timothy
  6:10

NT WORD 11. PHILARGUROS

Money-Loving

φιλάργυρος *fil-ar´-goo-ros*. From *philos* (*friendly, loving*) and *arguros* (*silver*). Adjective. *Fond of silver, money-loving.* Strong's: G 5366.

Philarguros means *greedy for money, avaricious,* and *covetous.* This word describes a dishonest person who is unethical and uncharitable in financial dealings.

Jesus spoke a parable to the Pharisees about faithfulness in the stewardship of money. Their response? They *derided* Him. (See Luke 16:14) In Greek, "deride" is a strong word, meaning *to sneer, scoff at,* or *turn up the nose with contempt.* Their intense reaction proved that Jesus' words exposed the stronghold of money love in their hearts.

Philarguros is one aspect of the extreme self-love that characterizes unsaved men in the last days. (See 2 Tim. 3:2)

In contrast, there is a word with the opposite sense, *aphilarguros*, which means *un-money-loving*. It is translated as "not greedy for money" in 1 Timothy 3:3 and is a qualification of Christian elders. In Hebrews 13:5, *aphilarguros* is translated "without covetousness." That verse urges us to "be content with such things as [we] have." With the Holy Spirit's help, we will not be driven by greed.

≔ TRANSLATION TALLY

lovers of money   2   times   See *You and God*

 **YOU AND GOD**

Luke
16:14 (10–15)

2 Timothy
3:2 (1–5)

NT WORD 12. PHILAUTOS

Self-Loving

φίλαυτος *fil´-ow-tos*. From *philos* (*friendly, loving*) and *autos* (*self*). Adjective. *Self-loving*. Strong's: G 5367

Philautos speaks of those who are *selfish,* self-centered, self-serving, self-exalting, self-indulgent, and idolatrous (in placing love of self before love for God). Extreme selfishness will characterize unsaved people in these last days. Contrast Matt. 16:24, Luke 14:8–11, John 3:30, 1 Cor. 13:5b, Phil. 2:4–8, 19–21.

☷ Translation Tally

lovers of themselves   1   time   See *You and God*

 You and God

2 Timothy
  3:2 (1–5)

NT WORD 13. PHILEDONOS

Pleasure-Loving

φιλήδονος fil-ay´-don-os. From *philos* (*friendly, loving*) and *hedone* (*sensual pleasure* or the *desire* for it; *hedone* is found in Luke 8:14, Titus 3:3, James 4:1, 3, 2 Peter 2:13). Adjective. *Pleasure-loving, hedonistic.* Strong's: G 5369.

Philedonos refers to *one given over to the pursuit of sensual pleasure, a pleasure seeker,* or *a thrill seeker.* It describes the unbridled sensuality and excesses of worldliness that distinguish the unsaved in the last days. (Titus 3:3, 2 Peter 2:13) This driving thirst for personal pleasure (called by the rabbis the "evil impulse") is opposed to God, chokes His Word (Luke 8:14), wars against the Christian soul (James 4:1–2, 1 Peter 2:11), causes fights and conflicts in the church (James 4:1–2), and perverts prayer. (James 4:3)

In 2 Timothy 3:4, the *pleasure lover* is classed with the *self lover* (Word 12), the *money lover* (Word 11), and other ungodly characteristics. The *pleasure lover* is contrasted with the *God lover* (Word 17). The latter puts to death the deeds of his flesh and keeps his bodily appetites under control as proof of his love for God. (Cp. John 14:15, 21, 23; Rom. 8:12–14, 1 Cor. 9:27) See Word 17. Philotheos.

≔ TRANSLATION TALLY

lovers of pleasure   1   time   See *You and God*

 YOU AND GOD

2 Timothy
3:4 (1–5)

NT WORD 14. PHILEO

Natural Human Love

φιλέω *fil-eh´-o.* From *philos* (*friendly, loving*). Verb. *To love.* Strong's: G 5368.

Phileo means *to have affection for, hold dear, cherish,* and *love* in an affectionate, warm, and friendly manner; *to be fond of, like,* or *delight in* a thing; also *to kiss.*

Scripture uses *phileo* in two distinct ways: (1) as natural human love for the people, things, and activities of this world, such as parents, children, the best places at feasts, one's life in this world, and even to cherish a lie; and (2) as a spiritual love accompanied by feelings of deep tenderness, especially of the tender affection of the Father for Jesus (John 5:20) and His disciples (John 16:27), of Jesus' love for His disciples (John 11:3, 36, 20:2, Rev. 3:19), and of the disciples' love for their Lord and each other. (1 Cor. 16:22, Titus 3:15)

Phileo is the common emotion of love based on natural affection, likeability, friendship, having things in common, and mutual response. *Agapao* (Word 1) signifies an *unconditional* decision to love, regardless of natural attraction or response.

Before the writing of the New Testament, *phileo* was the common Greek verb for human affection, friendship, and love. Because of its well-established meaning, it was not a suitable vehicle to express the supernatural love sourced in God. Instead, the Holy Spirit chose the relatively rare (and less defined) *agapao/agape* word group for that purpose. (See Words 1 and 2.)

☰ TRANSLATION TALLY

kiss	3	times	Mt 26:48, Mk 14:44, Lk 22:47
love	13	"	See *You and God*
loved	3	"	" " "
loves	6	"	" " "

YOU AND GOD

Matthew
  6:5 (5–6)
  10:37 (34–39)
  23:6 (5–8)
Luke
  20:46 (45–47)

John
  5:20 (16–21)
  11:3 (1–5)
  11:36 (32–38)
  12:25 (23–26)
  15:19 (16–19)
  16:27 (23–28)

  20:2 (1–4)
  21:15, 16, 17 (13–17)
1 Corinthians
  16:22 (19–24)
Titus
  3:15 (12–15)

Revelation
  3:19 (17–20)
  22:15 (12–16)

NT WORD 15. PHILOPROTEUO

Power-Loving

φιλοπρωτεύω *fil-op-rote-yoo´-o*. From *philoprotos*, a compound of *philos* (*friendly, loving*) and *protos* (*first in rank, foremost, chief*). Verb. *To love to be first, to strive for preeminence.* Strong's: G 5383.

In his third epistle, the apostle John rebuked a certain Diotrephes. This self-styled church leader rejected John's apostolic authority, spoke against him, and refused to offer hospitality to the missionary brothers John sent. (Cp. John 13:20) In describing Diotrephes as *philoproteuo*, John pointed to selfish ambition as the moral flaw in his character, which prevented his continuing as an elder.

Philoproteuo is lust for preeminence and power. Rejection of the authority of another characterizes this desire to control, take over, and rule. The same sin led Korah to rebel against Moses. In ironic justice, *only* those who rebelled against Moses' command to get away from the tents of Korah, Dathan, and Abiram perished when the earth opened and swallowed them. (Numbers 16)

Korah's rebellion originated in the same lust for prominence, prestige, and worship the angel Lucifer exhibited when he said, "I will be like the Most High." (Isa. 14:14) As a result, God tossed him out of heaven, and he became Satan, the "most low" devil. (Isa. 14:15, Luke 10:18)

As in the Old Testament, some in New Testament congregations succumb to pride, selfish ambition, and rivalry. (Gal. 5:20, 1 Tim. 3:6) They seek to manipulate or rise against the leaders God appointed in the church. John and his brother James had to overcome this same desire for prominence themselves, as recorded in Mark 10:35–45. In identifying Diotrephes' love to be in the forefront, John knew of which he spoke.

In the Church, only Jesus is preeminent. (Col. 1:18) As the head of the Church, Jesus appoints leaders as gifts to His body. He sets qualified people into offices of leadership and authority, not as lords but examples. (Eph. 4:11–13, 1 Peter 5:2–3) Those who submit to church leaders in faith that God will work through them are blessed. Those who criticize, complain, rebel, and pull away disqualify themselves from leadership.

Recognizing and submitting to God-ordained authority is a necessary part of leadership training. This may require healing from unresolved past hurts, painful authority issues, and roots of bitterness. It is tragic when talented, gifted individuals cannot submit to godly authority, frustrating and forfeiting God's plan for their lives.

≣ Translation Tally

loves to have the preeminence	1 time	See *You and God*

 You and God

3 John :9 (9–12)

NT WORD 16. PHILOTEKNOS

Children-Loving

φιλότεκνος *fil-ot'-ek-nos*. From *philos* (*friendly, loving*) and *teknon* (*child*). Adjective. *Loving children.* Strong's: G 5388.

Philoteknos is a vital instruction to be imparted by mature Christian ladies to the younger ones. Next to loving their husbands (see Word 8. Philandros), women are to *love their children* with warmth and affection. (1 Thess. 2:7) That includes bringing them up in the "training and admonition of the Lord." (Eph. 6:4)

According to the Bible, the father is primarily responsible for instructing children in the ways of God. (Deut. 6:1–7, Eph. 6:4) But Proverbs mentions the mother's contribution. (Prov. 1:8, 6:20, 23:22, 30:17, 31:1) Paul commended Timothy's mother and grandmother for communicating their genuine faith to Timothy. (2 Tim. 1:5 with 3:15)

A Christian mother's goodness, love, faith, care, and ongoing prayers leave an indelible impression on her children, grandchildren, great-grandchildren, adopted children, and spiritual children. A mother's love provides the basis for a moral argument that there is a God and that He is good.

We must never underestimate the godly influence loving Christian mothers, grandmothers, and great-grandmothers have on their families, and thus on society. Theirs is a world-changing ministry because mothers affect every human being on earth. This planet would be better if a true mother's love graced every person's life.

TRANSLATION TALLY

love their children   1   time   See *You and God*

YOU AND GOD

Titus 2:4 (1–6)

NT WORD 17. PHILOTHEOS

God-Loving

φιλόθεος *fil-oth´-eh-os.* From *philos* (*friendly, loving*) and *theos* (*God*). Adjective. *God-loving.* Strong's: G 5377.

Philotheos describes *those given over to the pursuit of God,* who do their best to love God with the totality of their being. They are sold out to the Lord and put God first in their lives.

In contrast, the apostasy of the last days is characterized by those who have an outward form of godliness but deny the regenerating power of God—not being born again. They profess to know God but deny Him in works. (Titus 1:16) They honor God with their lips, but their heart is far from Him (Mark 7:6). They are lovers of self, money, sensual pleasure, and the applause of men more than lovers of God. (John 12:42–43) They do not know God as the holy, wonderful Person He is.

We, as Christians, have a choice every day. Will we be God lovers or pleasure lovers? Will we walk our talk, or will we love the world and its things? We can tell what we value most by where we spend our free time. What are our minds, hearts, and attention drawn to? Pleasures? Hobbies? Recreational activities? Social media? Entertainment? Or to God, His Word, prayer, and personal worship? Is our devotion weeklong or merely a warm, Sunday-morning feeling?

Our culture has more amusements and opportunities for pleasure than any previous generation. Many of them are not sinful in themselves. Still, innocent pleasures, when overdone, sap our spiritual strength, steal our time, dilute our intensity, reduce our ability to recharge, and weaken our effectiveness. Why? They keep us away from godly disciplines. They are thorns in our good ground that choke the seed of the Word.

If we have committed our lives to serve the Lord Jesus Christ, then we must be *God lovers* in daily prayer, Bible reading, worship, witness, church attendance, self-denial, giving, patience, kindness, and mercy. A simple prayer is: *Father, I love you. Help me to love you more! Help me to love you with my lifestyle, not just in words or feelings. In Jesus' name. Amen.*

☰ TRANSLATION TALLY

lovers of God	1 time	See *You and God*

 YOU AND GOD

2 Timothy 3:4 (1–5)

NT WORD 18. PROSPHILES

Lovable

προσφιλής *pros-fee-lace´*. From *pros* (*towards*) and *phileo* (*to love,* Word 14). Adjective. *Lovable, lovely.* Strong's: G 4375.

Prosphiles describes something a person is *positively affectioned toward* and *kindly disposed to.* It is what is *pleasing, acceptable,* and *agreeable.*

In Philippians 4:8 where *prosphiles* is found, the apostle Paul shares the secrets to inner peace. They come from: (1) rejoicing in the Lord always; (2) rolling over on God in prayer whatever causes anxiety (1 Peter 5:7); and (3) meditating on things that are true, noble, just, pure, lovely (*prosphiles*), of good report, virtuous, and praiseworthy.

As human beings, we don't usually meditate on *things*. We meditate on *people* and what they've done to us, whether real or imagined. To think what is true, noble, just, pure, lovely, of good report, virtuous, and praiseworthy about people, we must forgive from the heart any harm they have done. (Matt. 18:21–35) Until we forgive, we can't think positively about them or experience peace. After we forgive, we see those who hurt us in a different light.

We have a daily (and sometimes, minute-by-minute) choice to meditate on our problems or the provision God made for us. Meditative thought patterns can spiral downward to negativity, discouragement, and despair or climb upward to faith and hope in God. When little seems encouraging in the natural, God will give you strength as you meditate on the Scripture promises of His marvelous grace and saving power.

God's Word is true, noble, just, pure, lovely, of good report, virtuous, and praiseworthy! God can never lie, break His covenant, nor alter the Word that has gone out of His mouth. (Num. 23:19, Ps. 89:34) He gave His Word that "we through the patience and comfort of the Scriptures might have hope" (Rom. 15:4) and experience the presence of the God of peace.

⋮≡ TRANSLATION TALLY

lovely	1 time	See *You and God*

 YOU AND GOD

Philippians 4:8 (6–9)

NT WORD 19. THELO

To Want

θέλω *thel´-o*. Derivation uncertain. Verb. *To want, will, wish, desire,* specifically, *to take pleasure in, to like* to do. Strong's: G 2309.

Thelo is the primary Greek word for *willing, wishing, wanting,* and *desiring,* as seen in the Translation Tally. It speaks of the will proceeding from one's inclination, preference, and liking.

In Mark 12:38, the word *"love"* appears in italics as a word supplied by translators. However, *love* is implied from *thelo,* the preceding verb translated as "desire." *Thelo* is also suggested by the parallel passage in Luke 20:46, which contains both *thelo* and *phileo* (Word 14).

Jesus condemned the scribes for delighting in outward shows of piety, such as *loving* to wear long robes and sit in prominent places in the synagogues, while being destitute of a character pleasing to God.

≔ TRANSLATION TALLY

delight, taking	1	time(s)	Col 2:18
desire	41	"	Mt 9:13, 12:7, 15:28, etc.
desire, might	1	"	2 Cor 12:6
desiring, be	1	"	2 Cor 8:10
intending	2	"	Lk 14:28, Acts 14:13
love	1	"	See *You and God*
mean	2	"	Acts 2:12, 17:20
please	2	"	1 Cor 12:18, 15:38
refusing (+ *ou* [not])	1	"	Mt 2:18
want	80	"	Mt 1:19, 5:40, 42, 7:12, etc.
will	18	"	Mt 21:29, 23:4, 26:39, etc.
will have	1	"	Mt 27:43
will to do	5	"	Rom 7:15, 16, 19, 20
willfully	1	"	2 Pe 3:5
willing	1	"	Acts 18:21
willing, be	15	"	Mt 8:2, 3, 11:14, 22:3, etc.
willingly	1	"	John 6:21
wish	24	"	Mt 17:4, 12, 20:14, 15, 21, etc.
would	9	"	Mt 18:30, 27:34, Mk 6:48, etc.

would like	1	"	Gal 4:20
would rather	1	"	1 Cor 14:19

 YOU AND GOD

Mark 12:38 (38–40)

He who does not love does not know God,
for God is love.

—1 John 4:8

The New Testament Verse Concordance

Every Use of
Any Form of
The Word LOVE

Including...
*Beloved, Love, Loved, Lovely,
Lover, Lovers, Love's, Loves,
Unloving*

And this is His commandment: that we should believe on the name of His Son Jesus Christ and love one another, as He gave us commandment.

—1 John 3:23

NEW TESTAMENT VERSE CONCORDANCE

For the meaning and usage of the Greek words in bold print, refer to the corresponding New Testament Word Sections. The Old Testament Verse Concordance begins on page 159.

The following Scriptures are taken from the New King James Version®. Copyright © 1982 by Thomas Nelson. Used by permission. All rights reserved.

❏ Matthew

3:17	And suddenly a voice *came* from heaven, saying, "This is My **beloved [3. agapetos]**...Son, in whom I am well pleased."
5:43	"You have heard that it was said, 'You shall **love [1. agapao]**...your neighbor and hate your enemy.' "
5:44	"But I say to you, **love [1. agapao]**...your enemies, bless those who curse you, do good to those who hate you, and pray for those who spitefully use you and persecute you,"
5:46	"For if you **love [1. agapao]**...those who **love [1. agapao]**...you, what reward have you? Do not even the tax collectors do the same?"
6: 5	"And when you pray, you shall not be like the hypocrites. For they **love [14. phileo]**...to pray standing in the synagogues and on the corners of the streets, that they may be seen by men. Assuredly, I say to you, they have their reward."
6:24	"No one can serve two masters; for either he will hate the one and **love [1. agapao]**...the other, or else he will be loyal to the one and despise the other. You cannot serve God and mammon."
10:37	"He who **loves [14. phileo]**...father or mother more than Me is not worthy of Me. And he who **loves [14. phileo]**...son or daughter more than Me is not worthy of Me."
12:18	"Behold! My Servant whom I have chosen, My **Beloved [3. agapetos]**...in whom My soul is well pleased! I will put My Spirit upon Him, And He will declare justice to the Gentiles."
17: 5	While he was still speaking, behold, a bright cloud overshadowed them; and suddenly a voice came out of the cloud, saying, "This is My **beloved [3. agapetos]**...Son, in whom I am well pleased. Hear Him!"

LOVE THROUGHOUT THE NEW TESTAMENT / 99

19:19	" 'Honor your father and your mother,' and, 'You shall **love** [1. agapao]...your neighbor as yourself.' "
22:37	Jesus said to him, " 'You shall **love** [1. agapao]...the LORD your God with all your heart, with all your soul, and with all your mind.' "
22:39	"And *the* second *is* like it: 'You shall **love** [1. agapao]...your neighbor as yourself.' "
23: 6	"They **love** [14. phileo]...the best places at feasts, the best seats in the synagogues,"
24:12	"And because lawlessness will abound, the **love** [2. agape]...of many will grow cold."

❏ Mark

1:11	Then a voice came from heaven, "You are My **beloved** [3. agapetos]...Son, in whom I am well pleased."
9: 7	And a cloud came and overshadowed them; and a voice came out of the cloud, saying, "This is My **beloved** [3. agapetos]...Son. Hear Him!"
10:21	Then Jesus, looking at him, **loved** [1. agapao]...him, and said to him, "One thing you lack: Go your way, sell whatever you have and give to the poor, and you will have treasure in heaven; and come, take up the cross, and follow Me."
12: 6	"Therefore still having one son, his...**beloved** [3. agapetos], he also sent him to them last, saying, 'They will respect my son.' "
12:30	" 'And you shall **love** [1. agapao]...the LORD your God with all your heart, with all your soul, with all your mind, and with all your strength.' This *is* the first commandment."
12:31	"And the second, like *it, is* this: 'You shall **love** [1. agapao]...your neighbor as yourself.' There is no other commandment greater than these."
12:33	"And to **love** [1. agapao]...Him with all the heart, with all the understanding, with all the soul, and with all the strength, and to **love** [1. agapao]...one's neighbor as oneself, is more than all the whole burnt offerings and sacrifices."
12:38	Then He said to them in His teaching, "Beware of the scribes, who desire to go around in long robes, *love* [19. thelo]...greetings in the marketplaces,"

❏ Luke

3:22	And the Holy Spirit descended in bodily form like a dove upon Him, and a voice came from heaven which said, "You are My **beloved** [3. agapetos]...Son; in You I am well pleased."

6:27	"But I say to you who hear: **Love [1. agapao]**...your enemies, do good to those who hate you,"
6:32	"But if you **love [1. agapao]**...those who **love [1. agapao]**...you, what credit is that to you? For even sinners **love [1. agapao]**...those who **love [1. agapao]**...them."
6:35	"But **love [1. agapao]**...your enemies, do good, and lend, hoping for nothing in return; and your reward will be great, and you will be sons of the Most High. For He is kind to the unthankful and evil."
7: 5	"for he **loves [1. agapao]**...our nation, and has built us a synagogue."
7:42	"And when they had nothing with which to repay, he freely forgave them both. Tell Me, therefore, which of them will **love [1. agapao]**...him more?"
7:47	"Therefore I say to you, her sins, *which are* many, are forgiven, for she **loved [1. agapao]**...much. But to whom little is forgiven, *the same* **loves [1. agapao]**...little."
9:35	And a voice came out of the cloud, saying, "This is My **beloved [3. agapetos]**...Son. Hear Him!"
10:27	So he answered and said, " 'You shall **love [1. agapao]**...the LORD your God with all your heart, with all your soul, with all your strength, and with all your mind,' and 'your neighbor as yourself.' "
11:42	"But woe to you Pharisees! For you tithe mint and rue and all manner of herbs, and pass by justice and the **love [2. agape]**...of God. These you ought to have done, without leaving the others undone."
11:43	"Woe to you Pharisees! For you **love [1. agapao]**...the best seats in the synagogues and greetings in the marketplaces."
16:13	"No servant can serve two masters; for either he will hate the one and **love [1. agapao]**...the other, or else he will be loyal to the one and despise the other. You cannot serve God and mammon."
16:14	Now the Pharisees, who were...**lovers of money [11. philarguros]**, also heard all these things, and they derided Him.
20:13	"Then the owner of the vineyard said, 'What shall I do? I will send my **beloved [3. agapetos]**...son. Probably they will respect *him* when they see him.' "
20:46	"Beware of the scribes, who desire to go around in long robes, **love [14. phileo]**...greetings in the marketplaces, the best seats in the synagogues, and the best places at feasts,"

❏ John

3:16	"For God so **loved [1. agapao]**...the world that He gave His only begotten Son, that whoever believes in Him should not perish but have everlasting life."

3:19	"And this is the condemnation, that the light has come into the world, and men **loved [1. agapao]**...darkness rather than light, because their deeds were evil."
3:35	"The Father **loves [1. agapao]**...the Son, and has given all things into His hand."
5:20	"For the Father **loves [14. phileo]**...the Son, and shows Him all things that He Himself does; and He will show Him greater works than these, that you may marvel."
5:42	"But I know you, that you do not have the **love [2. agape]**...of God in you."
8:42	Jesus said to them, "If God were your Father, you would **love [1. agapao]**...Me, for I proceeded forth and came from God; nor have I come of Myself, but He sent Me."
10:17	"Therefore My Father **loves [1. agapao]**...Me, because I lay down My life that I may take it again."
11: 3	Therefore the sisters sent to Him, saying, "Lord, behold, he whom You **love [14. phileo]**...is sick."
11: 5	Now Jesus **loved [1. agapao]**...Martha and her sister and Lazarus.
11:36	Then the Jews said, "See how He **loved [14. phileo]**...him!"
12:25	"He who **loves [14. phileo]**...his life will lose it, and he who hates his life in this world will keep it for eternal life."
12:43	for they **loved [1. agapao]**...the praise of men more than the praise of God.
13: 1	Now before the feast of the Passover, when Jesus knew that His hour had come that He should depart from this world to the Father, having **loved [1. agapao]**...His own who were in the world, He **loved [1. agapao]**...them to the end.
13:23	Now there was leaning on Jesus' bosom one of His disciples, whom Jesus... **loved [1. agapao]**.
13:34	"A new commandment I give to you, that you **love [1. agapao]**...one another; as I have **loved [1. agapao]**...you, that you also **love [1. agapao]**...one another."
13:35	"By this all will know that you are My disciples, if you have **love [2. agape]**...for one another."
14:15	"If you **love [1. agapao]**...Me, keep My commandments."
14:21	"He who has My commandments and keeps them, it is he who **loves [1. agapao]**...Me. And he who **loves [1. agapao]**...Me will be **loved [1. agapao]**...by My Father, and I will **love [1. agapao]**...him and manifest Myself to him."

14:23	Jesus answered and said to him, "If anyone **loves** [**1. agapao**]…Me, he will keep My word; and My Father will **love** [**1. agapao**]…him, and We will come to him and make Our home with him."
14:24	"He who does not **love** [**1. agapao**]…Me does not keep My words; and the word which you hear is not Mine but the Father's who sent Me."
14:28	"You have heard Me say to you, 'I am going away and coming back to you.' If you **loved** [**1. agapao**]…Me, you would rejoice because I said, 'I am going to the Father,' for My Father is greater than I."
14:31	"But that the world may know that I **love** [**1. agapao**]…the Father, and as the Father gave Me commandment, so I do. Arise, let us go from here."
15: 9	"As the Father **loved** [**1. agapao**]…Me, I also have **loved** [**1. agapao**]…you; abide in My…**love** [**2. agape**]."
15:10	"If you keep My commandments, you will abide in My…**love** [**2. agape**], just as I have kept My Father's commandments and abide in His…**love** [**2. agape**]."
15:12	"This is My commandment, that you **love** [**1. agapao**]…one another as I have **loved** [**1. agapao**]…you."
15:13	"Greater **love** [**2. agape**]…has no one than this, than to lay down one's life for his friends."
15:17	"These things I command you, that you **love** [**1. agapao**]…one another."
15:19	"If you were of the world, the world would **love** [**14. phileo**]…its own. Yet because you are not of the world, but I chose you out of the world, therefore the world hates you."
16:27	"for the Father Himself **loves** [**14. phileo**]…you, because you have **loved** [**14. phileo**]…Me, and have believed that I came forth from God."
17:23	"I in them, and You in Me; that they may be made perfect in one, and that the world may know that You have sent Me, and have **loved** [**1. agapao**]…them as You have **loved** [**1. agapao**]…Me."
17:24	"Father, I desire that they also whom You gave Me may be with Me where I am, that they may behold My glory which You have given Me; for You **loved** [**1. agapao**]…Me before the foundation of the world."
17:26	"And I have declared to them Your name, and will declare *it,* that the **love** [**2. agape**]…with which You **loved** [**1. agapao**]…Me may be in them, and I in them."
19:26	When Jesus therefore saw His mother, and the disciple whom He **loved** [**1. agapao**]…standing by, He said to His mother, "Woman, behold your son!"
20: 2	Then she ran and came to Simon Peter, and to the other disciple, whom Jesus…**loved** [**14. phileo**], and said to them, "They have taken away the Lord out of the tomb, and we do not know where they have laid Him."

21: 7	Therefore that disciple whom Jesus **loved [1. agapao]**...said to Peter, "It is the Lord!" Now when Simon Peter heard that it was the Lord, he put on *his* outer garment (for he had removed it), and plunged into the sea.
21:15	So when they had eaten breakfast, Jesus said to Simon Peter, "Simon, *son* of Jonah, do you **love [1. agapao]**...Me more than these?" He said to Him, "Yes, Lord; You know that I **love [14. phileo]**...You." He said to him, "Feed My lambs."
21:16	He said to him again a second time, "Simon, *son* of Jonah, do you **love [1. agapao]**...Me?" He said to Him, "Yes, Lord; You know that I **love [14. phileo]**...You." He said to him, "Tend My sheep."
21:17	He said to him the third time, "Simon, *son* of Jonah, do you **love [14. phileo]**...Me?" Peter was grieved because He said to him the third time, "Do you **love [14. phileo]**...Me?" And he said to Him, "Lord, You know all things; You know that I **love [14. phileo]**...You." Jesus said to him, "Feed My sheep."
21:20	Then Peter, turning around, saw the disciple whom Jesus **loved [1. agapao]**...following, who also had leaned on His breast at the supper, and said, "Lord, who is the one who betrays You?"

❏ Acts

15:25	It seemed good to us, being assembled with one accord, to send chosen men to you with our **beloved [3. agapetos]**...Barnabas and Paul,

❏ Romans

1: 7	To all who are in Rome, **beloved [3. agapetos]**...of God, called *to be* saints: Grace to you and peace from God our Father and the Lord Jesus Christ.
1:31	undiscerning, untrustworthy, **unloving [4. astorgos]**, unforgiving, unmerciful;
5: 5	Now hope does not disappoint, because the **love [2. agape]**...of God has been poured out in our hearts by the Holy Spirit who was given to us.
5: 8	But God demonstrates His own **love [2. agape]**...toward us, in that while we were still sinners, Christ died for us.
8:28	And we know that all things work together for good to those who **love [1. agapao]**...God, to those who are the called according to *His* purpose.
8:35	Who shall separate us from the **love [2. agape]**...of Christ? *Shall* tribulation, or distress, or persecution, or famine, or nakedness, or peril, or sword?
8:37	Yet in all these things we are more than conquerors through Him who **loved [1. agapao]**...us.

8:39	nor height nor depth, nor any other created thing, shall be able to separate us from the **love [2. agape]**...of God which is in Christ Jesus our Lord.
9:13	As it is written, "Jacob I have...**loved [1. agapao]**, but Esau I have hated."
9:25	As He says also in Hosea: "I will call them My people, who were not My people, And her...**beloved [1. agapao]**, who was not...**beloved [1. agapao]**."
11:28	Concerning the gospel *they are* enemies for your sake, but concerning the election *they are* **beloved [3. agapetos]**...for the sake of the fathers.
12:9	*Let* **love [2. agape]**...*be* without hypocrisy. Abhor what is evil. Cling to what is good.
12:10	*Be* kindly affectionate to one another with...**brotherly love [5. philadelphia]**, in honor giving preference to one another;
12:19	**Beloved [3. agapetos]**, do not avenge yourselves, but *rather* give place to wrath; for it is written, "Vengeance *is* Mine, I will repay," says the Lord.
13:8	Owe no one anything except to **love [1. agapao]**...one another, for he who **loves [1. agapao]**...another has fulfilled the law.
13:9	For the commandments, "You shall not commit adultery," "You shall not murder," "You shall not steal," "You shall not bear false witness," "You shall not covet," and if *there is* any other commandment, are *all* summed up in this saying, namely, "You shall **love [1. agapao]**...your neighbor as yourself."
13:10	**Love [2. agape]**...does no harm to a neighbor; therefore **love [2. agape]**...*is* the fulfillment of the law.
14:15	Yet if your brother is grieved because of *your* food, you are no longer walking in...**love [2. agape]**. Do not destroy with your food the one for whom Christ died.
15:30	Now I beg you, brethren, through the Lord Jesus Christ, and through the **love [2. agape]**...of the Spirit, that you strive together with me in prayers to God for me,
16:5	Likewise *greet* the church that is in their house. Greet my **beloved [3. agapetos]**...Epaenetus, who is the firstfruits of Achaia to Christ.
16:8	Greet Amplias, my **beloved [3. agapetos]**...in the Lord.
16:9	Greet Urbanus, our fellow worker in Christ, and Stachys, my...**beloved [3. agapetos]**.
16:12	Greet Tryphena and Tryphosa, who have labored in the Lord. Greet the **beloved [3. agapetos]**...Persis, who labored much in the Lord.

❏ 1 Corinthians

2: 9	But as it is written: "Eye has not seen, nor ear heard, Nor have entered into the heart of man The things which God has prepared for those who **love [1. agapao]**...Him."
4:14	I do not write these things to shame you, but as my **beloved [3. agapetos]**...children I warn *you*.
4:17	For this reason I have sent Timothy to you, who is my **beloved [3. agapetos]**...and faithful son in the Lord, who will remind you of my ways in Christ, as I teach everywhere in every church.
4:21	What do you want? Shall I come to you with a rod, or in **love [2. agape]**...and a spirit of gentleness?
8: 1	Now concerning things offered to idols: We know that we all have knowledge. Knowledge puffs up, but **love [2. agape]**...edifies.
8: 3	But if anyone **loves [1. agapao]**...God, this one is known by Him.
10:14	Therefore, my...**beloved [3. agapetos]**, flee from idolatry.
13: 1	Though I speak with the tongues of men and of angels, but have not...**love [2. agape]**, I have become sounding brass or a clanging cymbal.
13: 2	And though I have *the gift of* prophecy, and understand all mysteries and all knowledge, and though I have all faith, so that I could remove mountains, but have not...**love [2. agape]**, I am nothing.
13: 3	And though I bestow all my goods to feed *the poor,* and though I give my body to be burned, but have not...**love [2. agape]**, it profits me nothing.
13: 4	**Love [2. agape]**...suffers long *and* is kind; **love [2. agape]**...does not envy; **love [2. agape]**...does not parade itself, is not puffed up;
13: 8	**Love [2. agape]**...never fails. But whether *there are* prophecies, they will fail; whether *there are* tongues, they will cease; whether *there is* knowledge, it will vanish away.
13:13	And now abide faith, hope, **love [2. agape]**, these three; but the greatest of these *is*...**love [2. agape]**.
14: 1	Pursue...**love [2. agape]**, and desire spiritual *gifts,* but especially that you may prophesy.
15:58	Therefore, my **beloved [3. agapetos]**...brethren, be steadfast, immovable, always abounding in the work of the Lord, knowing that your labor is not in vain in the Lord.
16:14	Let all *that* you *do* be done with...**love [2. agape]**.

16:22	If anyone does not **love** [**14. phileo**]...the Lord Jesus Christ, let him be accursed. O Lord, come!
16:24	My **love** [**2. agape**]...*be* with you all in Christ Jesus. Amen.

❏ 2 Corinthians

2: 4	For out of much affliction and anguish of heart I wrote to you, with many tears, not that you should be grieved, but that you might know the **love** [**2. agape**]...which I have so abundantly for you.
2: 8	Therefore I urge you to reaffirm *your* **love** [**2. agape**]...to him.
5:14	For the **love** [**2. agape**]...of Christ compels us, because we judge thus: that if One died for all, then all died;
6: 6	by purity, by knowledge, by longsuffering, by kindness, by the Holy Spirit, by sincere...**love** [**2. agape**],
7: 1	Therefore, having these promises, **beloved** [**3. agapetos**], let us cleanse ourselves from all filthiness of the flesh and spirit, perfecting holiness in the fear of God.
8: 7	But as you abound in everything—in faith, in speech, in knowledge, in all diligence, and in your **love** [**2. agape**]...for us—*see* that you abound in this grace also.
8: 8	I speak not by commandment, but I am testing the sincerity of your **love** [**2. agape**]...by the diligence of others.
8:24	Therefore show to them, and before the churches, the proof of your **love** [**2. agape**]...and of our boasting on your behalf.
9: 7	*So let* each one *give* as he purposes in his heart, not grudgingly or of necessity; for God **loves** [**1. agapao**]...a cheerful giver.
11:11	Why? Because I do not **love** [**1. agapao**]...you? God knows!
12:15	And I will very gladly spend and be spent for your souls; though the more abundantly I **love** [**1. agapao**]...you, the less I am...**loved** [**1. agapao**].
12:19	Again, do you think that we excuse ourselves to you? We speak before God in Christ. But *we do* all things, **beloved** [**3. agapetos**], for your edification.
13:11	Finally, brethren, farewell. Become complete. Be of good comfort, be of one mind, live in peace; and the God of **love** [**2. agape**]...and peace will be with you.
13:14	The grace of the Lord Jesus Christ, and the **love** [**2. agape**]...of God, and the communion of the Holy Spirit *be* with you all. Amen.

❏ Galatians

2:20   "I have been crucified with Christ; it is no longer I who live, but Christ lives in me; and the *life* which I now live in the flesh I live by faith in the Son of God, who **loved [1. agapao]**...me and gave Himself for me."

5: 6   For in Christ Jesus neither circumcision nor uncircumcision avails anything, but faith working through...**love [2. agape]**.

5:13   For you, brethren, have been called to liberty; only do not *use* liberty as an opportunity for the flesh, but through **love [2. agape]**...serve one another.

5:14   For all the law is fulfilled in one word, *even* in this: "You shall **love [1. agapao]**...your neighbor as yourself."

5:22   But the fruit of the Spirit is...**love [2. agape]**, joy, peace, longsuffering, kindness, goodness, faithfulness,

❏ Ephesians

1: 4   just as He chose us in Him before the foundation of the world, that we should be holy and without blame before Him in...**love [2. agape]**,

1: 6   to the praise of the glory of His grace, by which He has made us accepted in the...**Beloved [1. agapao]**.

1:15   Therefore I also, after I heard of your faith in the Lord Jesus and your **love [2. agape]**...for all the saints,

2: 4   But God, who is rich in mercy, because of His great **love [2. agape]**...with which He **loved [1. agapao]**...us,

3:17   that Christ may dwell in your hearts through faith; that you, being rooted and grounded in...**love [2. agape]**,

3:19   to know the **love [2. agape]**...of Christ which passes knowledge; that you may be filled with all the fullness of God.

4: 2   with all lowliness and gentleness, with longsuffering, bearing with one another in...**love [2. agape]**,

4:15   but, speaking the truth in...**love [2. agape]**, may grow up in all things into Him who is the head—Christ—

4:16   from whom the whole body, joined and knit together by what every joint supplies, according to the effective working by which every part does its share, causes growth of the body for the edifying of itself in...**love [2. agape]**.

5: 2   And walk in...**love [2. agape]**, as Christ also has **loved [1. agapao]**...us and given Himself for us, an offering and a sacrifice to God for a sweet-smelling aroma.

5:25	Husbands, **love** [1. agapao]...your wives, just as Christ also **loved** [1. agapao]...the church and gave Himself for her,
5:28	So husbands ought to **love** [1. agapao]...their own wives as their own bodies; he who **loves** [1. agapao]...his wife **loves** [1. agapao]...himself.
5:33	Nevertheless let each one of you in particular so **love** [1. agapao]...his own wife as himself, and let the wife *see* that she respects *her* husband.
6:21	But that you also may know my affairs *and* how I am doing, Tychicus, a **beloved** [3. agapetos]...brother and faithful minister in the Lord, will make all things known to you;
6:23	Peace to the brethren, and **love** [2. agape]...with faith, from God the Father and the Lord Jesus Christ.
6:24	Grace *be* with all those who **love** [1. agapao]...our Lord Jesus Christ in sincerity. Amen.

❏ Philippians

1: 9	And this I pray, that your **love** [2. agape]...may abound still more and more in knowledge and all discernment,
1:17	but the latter out of...**love** [2. agape], knowing that I am appointed for the defense of the gospel.
2: 1	Therefore if *there is* any consolation in Christ, if any comfort of...**love** [2. agape], if any fellowship of the Spirit, if any affection and mercy,
2: 2	fulfill my joy by being like-minded, having the same...**love** [2. agape], *being* of one accord, of one mind.
2:12	Therefore, my...**beloved** [3. agapetos], as you have always obeyed, not as in my presence only, but now much more in my absence, work out your own salvation with fear and trembling;
4: 1	Therefore, my **beloved** [3. agapetos]...and longed-for brethren, my joy and crown, so stand fast in the Lord, **beloved** [3. agapetos].
4: 8	Finally, brethren, whatever things are true, whatever things *are* noble, whatever things *are* just, whatever things *are* pure, whatever things *are*...**lovely** [18. prosphiles], whatever things *are* of good report, if *there is* any virtue and if *there is* anything praiseworthy—meditate on these things.

❏ Colossians

1: 4	since we heard of your faith in Christ Jesus and of your **love** [2. agape]...for all the saints;
1: 8	who also declared to us your **love** [2. agape]...in the Spirit.

1:13		He has delivered us from the power of darkness and conveyed *us* into the kingdom of the Son of His…**love [2. agape]**,
2: 2		that their hearts may be encouraged, being knit together in…**love [2. agape]**, and *attaining* to all riches of the full assurance of understanding, to the knowledge of the mystery of God, both of the Father and of Christ,
3:12		Therefore, as *the* elect of God, holy and…**beloved [1. agapao]**, put on tender mercies, kindness, humility, meekness, longsuffering;
3:14		But above all these things put on…**love [2. agape]**, which is the bond of perfection.
3:19		Husbands, **love [1. agapao]**…your wives and do not be bitter toward them.
4: 7		Tychicus, a **beloved [3. agapetos]**…brother, faithful minister, and fellow servant in the Lord, will tell you all the news about me.
4: 9		with Onesimus, a faithful and **beloved [3. agapetos]**…brother, who is *one* of you. They will make known to you all things which *are happening* here.
4:14		Luke the **beloved [3. agapetos]**…physician and Demas greet you.

❏ 1 Thessalonians

1: 3		remembering without ceasing your work of faith, labor of…**love [2. agape]**, and patience of hope in our Lord Jesus Christ in the sight of our God and Father,
1: 4		Knowing, **beloved [1. agapao]**…brethren, your election by God.
3: 6		But now that Timothy has come to us from you, and brought us good news of your faith and…**love [2. agape]**, and that you always have good remembrance of us, greatly desiring to see us, as we also *to see* you—
3:12		And may the Lord make you increase and abound in **love [2. agape]**…to one another and to all, just as we *do* to you,
4: 9		But concerning **brotherly love [5. philadelphia]**…you have no need that I should write to you, for you yourselves are taught by God to **love [1. agapao]**…one another;
5: 8		But let us who are of the day be sober, putting on the breastplate of faith and…**love [2. agape]**, and *as* a helmet the hope of salvation.
5:13		and to esteem them very highly in **love [2. agape]**…for their work's sake. Be at peace among yourselves.

❏ 2 Thessalonians

1: 3		We are bound to thank God always for you, brethren, as it is fitting, because your faith grows exceedingly, and the **love [2. agape]**...of every one of you all abounds toward each other,
2:10		and with all unrighteous deception among those who perish, because they did not receive the **love [2. agape]**...of the truth, that they might be saved.
2:13		But we are bound to give thanks to God always for you, brethren **beloved [1. agapao]**...by the Lord, because God from the beginning chose you for salvation through sanctification by the Spirit and belief in the truth,
2:16		Now may our Lord Jesus Christ Himself, and our God and Father, who has **loved [1. agapao]**...us and given *us* everlasting consolation and good hope by grace,
3: 5		Now may the Lord direct your hearts into the **love [2. agape]**...of God and into the patience of Christ.

❏ 1 Timothy

1: 5		Now the purpose of the commandment is **love [2. agape]**...from a pure heart, *from* a good conscience, and *from* sincere faith,
1:14		And the grace of our Lord was exceedingly abundant, with faith and **love [2. agape]**...which are in Christ Jesus.
2:15		Nevertheless she will be saved in childbearing if they continue in faith, **love [2. agape]**, and holiness, with self-control.
4:12		Let no one despise your youth, but be an example to the believers in word, in conduct, in...**love [2. agape]**, in spirit, in faith, in purity.
6: 2		And those who have believing masters, let them not despise *them* because they are brethren, but rather serve *them* because those who are benefited are believers and...**beloved [3. agapetos]**. Teach and exhort these things.
6:10		For the **love of money [10. philarguria]**...is a root of all *kinds of* evil, for which some have strayed from the faith in their greediness, and pierced themselves through with many sorrows.
6:11		But you, O man of God, flee these things and pursue righteousness, godliness, faith, **love [2. agape]**, patience, gentleness.

❏ 2 Timothy

1: 2		To Timothy, a **beloved [3. agapetos]**...son: Grace, mercy, *and* peace from God the Father and Christ Jesus our Lord.

2 Timothy NEW TESTAMENT VERSE CONCORDANCE

1: 7		For God has not given us a spirit of fear, but of power and of **love [2. agape]**...and of a sound mind.
1:13		Hold fast the pattern of sound words which you have heard from me, in faith and **love [2. agape]**...which are in Christ Jesus.
2:22		Flee also youthful lusts; but pursue righteousness, faith, **love [2. agape]**, peace with those who call on the Lord out of a pure heart.
3: 2		For men will be...**lovers of themselves [12. philautos], lovers of money [11. philarguros]**, boasters, proud, blasphemers, disobedient to parents, unthankful, unholy,
3: 3		**unloving [4. astorgos]**, unforgiving, slanderers, without self-control, brutal, despisers of good,
3: 4		traitors, headstrong, haughty, **lovers of pleasure [13. philedonos]**...rather than...**lovers of God [17. philotheos]**,
3:10		But you have carefully followed my doctrine, manner of life, purpose, faith, longsuffering, **love [2. agape]**, perseverance,
4: 8		Finally, there is laid up for me the crown of righteousness, which the Lord, the righteous Judge, will give to me on that Day, and not to me only but also to all who have **loved [1. agapao]**...His appearing.
4:10		for Demas has forsaken me, having **loved [1. agapao]**...this present world, and has departed for Thessalonica—Crescens for Galatia, Titus for Dalmatia.

❏ Titus

1: 8		but hospitable, **a lover of what is good [7. philagathos]**, sober-minded, just, holy, self-controlled,
2: 2		that the older men be sober, reverent, temperate, sound in faith, in... **love [2. agape]**, in patience;
2: 4		that they admonish the young women to...**love their husbands [8. philandros]**, to...**love their children [16. philoteknos]**,
3: 4		But when the kindness and the **love**...of God our Savior **toward man [9. philanthropia]**...appeared,
3:15		All who *are* with me greet you. Greet those who **love [14. phileo]**...us in the faith. Grace *be* with you all. Amen.

❏ Philemon

: 1		Paul, a prisoner of Christ Jesus, and Timothy *our* brother,
		To Philemon our **beloved [3. agapetos]**...*friend* and fellow laborer,

: 2	to the **beloved** [3. agapetos]…Apphia, Archippus our fellow soldier, and to the church in your house:
: 5	hearing of your **love** [2. agape]…and faith which you have toward the Lord Jesus and toward all the saints,
: 7	For we have great joy and consolation in your…**love** [2. agape], because the hearts of the saints have been refreshed by you, brother.
: 9	*yet* for **love's** [2. agape]…sake I rather appeal *to you*—being such a one as Paul, the aged, and now also a prisoner of Jesus Christ—
:16	no longer as a slave but more than a slave—a **beloved** [3. agapetos]… brother, especially to me but how much more to you, both in the flesh and in the Lord.

❏ Hebrews

1: 9	"You have **loved** [1. agapao]…righteousness and hated lawlessness; Therefore God, Your God, has anointed You With the oil of gladness more than Your companions."
6: 9	But, **beloved** [3. agapetos], we are confident of better things concerning you, yes, things that accompany salvation, though we speak in this manner.
6:10	For God *is* not unjust to forget your work and labor of **love** [2. agape]… which you have shown toward His name, *in that* you have ministered to the saints, and do minister.
10:24	And let us consider one another in order to stir up **love** [2. agape]…and good works,
12: 6	"For whom the LORD **loves** [1. agapao]…He chastens, And scourges every son whom He receives."
13: 1	Let **brotherly love** [5. philadelphia]…continue.

❏ James

1:12	Blessed *is* the man who endures temptation; for when he has been approved, he will receive the crown of life which the Lord has promised to those who **love** [1. agapao]…Him.
1:16	Do not be deceived, my **beloved** [3. agapetos]…brethren.
1:19	So then, my **beloved** [3. agapetos]…brethren, let every man be swift to hear, slow to speak, slow to wrath;
2: 5	Listen, my **beloved** [3. agapetos]…brethren: Has God not chosen the poor of this world *to be* rich in faith and heirs of the kingdom which He promised to those who **love** [1. agapao]…Him?

	2: 8	If you really fulfill *the* royal law according to the Scripture, "You shall **love [1. agapao]**...your neighbor as yourself," you do well;

❏ 1 Peter

	1: 8	whom having not seen you...**love [1. agapao]**. Though now you do not see *Him,* yet believing, you rejoice with joy inexpressible and full of glory,
	1:22	Since you have purified your souls in obeying the truth through the Spirit in sincere...**love of the brethren [5. philadelphia]**, **love [1. agapao]**...one another fervently with a pure heart,
	2:11	**Beloved [3. agapetos]**, I beg *you* as sojourners and pilgrims, abstain from fleshly lusts which war against the soul,
	2:17	Honor all *people*. **Love [1. agapao]**...the brotherhood. Fear God. Honor the king.
	3: 8	Finally, all *of you be* of one mind, having compassion for one another; **love as brothers [6. philadelphos]**, *be* tenderhearted, *be* courteous;
	3:10	For

> "He who would **love [1. agapao]**...life
> And see good days,
> Let him refrain his tongue from evil,
> And his lips from speaking deceit." |
	4: 8	And above all things have fervent **love [2. agape]**...for one another, for "**love [2. agape]**...will cover a multitude of sins."
	4:12	**Beloved [3. agapetos]**, do not think it strange concerning the fiery trial which is to try you, as though some strange thing happened to you;
	5:14	Greet one another with a kiss of...**love [2. agape]**. Peace to you all who are in Christ Jesus. Amen.

❏ 2 Peter

	1: 7	to godliness brotherly kindness, and to brotherly kindness...**love [2. agape]**.
	1:17	For He received from God the Father honor and glory when such a voice came to Him from the Excellent Glory: "This is My **beloved [3. agapetos]**...Son, in whom I am well pleased."
	2:15	They have forsaken the right way and gone astray, following the way of Balaam the *son* of Beor, who **loved [1. agapao]**...the wages of unrighteousness;
	3: 1	**Beloved [3. agapetos]**, I now write to you this second epistle (in *both of* which I stir up your pure minds by way of reminder),

3: 8	But, **beloved** [3. **agapetos**], do not forget this one thing, that with the Lord one day *is* as a thousand years, and a thousand years as one day.
3:14	Therefore, **beloved** [3. **agapetos**], looking forward to these things, be diligent to be found by Him in peace, without spot and blameless;
3:15	And consider *that* the longsuffering of our Lord *is* salvation—as also our **beloved** [3. **agapetos**]...brother Paul, according to the wisdom given to him, has written to you,
3:17	You therefore, **beloved** [3. **agapetos**], since you know *this* beforehand, beware lest you also fall from your own steadfastness, being led away with the error of the wicked;

❏ 1 John

2: 5	But whoever keeps His word, truly the **love** [2. **agape**]...of God is perfected in him. By this we know that we are in Him.
2:10	He who **loves** [1. **agapao**]...his brother abides in the light, and there is no cause for stumbling in him.
2:15	Do not **love** [1. **agapao**]...the world or the things in the world. If anyone **loves** [1. **agapao**]...the world, the **love** [2. **agape**]...of the Father is not in him.
3: 1	Behold what manner of **love** [2. **agape**]...the Father has bestowed on us, that we should be called children of God! Therefore the world does not know us, because it did not know Him.
3: 2	**Beloved** [3. **agapetos**], now we are children of God; and it has not yet been revealed what we shall be, but we know that when He is revealed, we shall be like Him, for we shall see Him as He is.
3:10	In this the children of God and the children of the devil are manifest: Whoever does not practice righteousness is not of God, nor *is* he who does not **love** [1. **agapao**]...his brother.
3:11	For this is the message that you heard from the beginning, that we should **love** [1. **agapao**]...one another,
3:14	We know that we have passed from death to life, because we **love** [1. **agapao**]...the brethren. He who does not **love** [1. **agapao**]...*his* brother abides in death.
3:16	By this we know...**love** [2. **agape**], because He laid down His life for us. And we also ought to lay down *our* lives for the brethren.
3:17	But whoever has this world's goods, and sees his brother in need, and shuts up his heart from him, how does the **love** [2. **agape**]...of God abide in him?
3:18	My little children, let us not **love** [1. **agapao**]...in word or in tongue, but in deed and in truth.

3:21	**Beloved [3. agapetos]**, if our heart does not condemn us, we have confidence toward God.
3:23	And this is His commandment: that we should believe on the name of His Son Jesus Christ and **love [1. agapao]**…one another, as He gave us commandment.
4: 1	**Beloved [3. agapetos]**, do not believe every spirit, but test the spirits, whether they are of God; because many false prophets have gone out into the world.
4: 7	**Beloved [3. agapetos]**, let us **love [1. agapao]**…one another, for **love [2. agape]**…is of God; and everyone who **loves [1. agapao]**…is born of God and knows God.
4: 8	He who does not **love [1. agapao]**…does not know God, for God is…**love [2. agape]**.
4: 9	In this the **love [2. agape]**…of God was manifested toward us, that God has sent His only begotten Son into the world, that we might live through Him.
4:10	In this is…**love [2. agape]**, not that we **loved [1. agapao]**…God, but that He **loved [1. agapao]**…us and sent His Son *to be* the propitiation for our sins.
4:11	**Beloved [3. agapetos]**, if God so **loved [1. agapao]**…us, we also ought to **love [1. agapao]**…one another.
4:12	No one has seen God at any time. If we **love [1. agapao]**…one another, God abides in us, and His **love [2. agape]**…has been perfected in us.
4:16	And we have known and believed the **love [2. agape]**…that God has for us. God is…**love [2. agape]**, and he who abides in **love [2. agape]**…abides in God, and God in him.
4:17	**Love [2. agape]**…has been perfected among us in this: that we may have boldness in the day of judgment; because as He is, so are we in this world.
4:18	There is no fear in…**love [2. agape]**; but perfect **love [2. agape]**…casts out fear, because fear involves torment. But he who fears has not been made perfect in…**love [2. agape]**.
4:19	We **love [1. agapao]**…Him because He first **loved [1. agapao]**…us.
4:20	If someone says, "I **love [1. agapao]**…God," and hates his brother, he is a liar; for he who does not **love [1. agapao]**…his brother whom he has seen, how can he **love [1. agapao]**…God whom he has not seen?
4:21	And this commandment we have from Him: that he who **loves [1. agapao]**…God *must* **love [1. agapao]**…his brother also.
5: 1	Whoever believes that Jesus is the Christ is born of God, and everyone who **loves [1. agapao]**…Him who begot also **loves [1. agapao]**…him who is begotten of Him.

5: 2   By this we know that we **love [1. agapao]**...the children of God, when we **love [1. agapao]**...God and keep His commandments.

5: 3   For this is the **love [2. agape]**...of God, that we keep His commandments. And His commandments are not burdensome.

❏ 2 John

: 1   The Elder,

       To the elect lady and her children, whom I **love [1. agapao]**...in truth, and not only I, but also all those who have known the truth,

: 3   Grace, mercy, *and* peace will be with you from God the Father and from the Lord Jesus Christ, the Son of the Father, in truth and...**love [2. agape]**.

: 5   And now I plead with you, lady, not as though I wrote a new commandment to you, but that which we have had from the beginning: that we **love [1. agapao]**...one another.

: 6   This is...**love [2. agape]**, that we walk according to His commandments. This is the commandment, that as you have heard from the beginning, you should walk in it.

❏ 3 John

: 1   The Elder,

       To the **beloved [3. agapetos]**...Gaius, whom I **love [1. agapao]**...in truth:

: 2   **Beloved [3. agapetos]**, I pray that you may prosper in all things and be in health, just as your soul prospers.

: 5   **Beloved [3. agapetos]**, you do faithfully whatever you do for the brethren and for strangers,

: 6   who have borne witness of your **love [2. agape]**...before the church. *If* you send them forward on their journey in a manner worthy of God, you will do well,

: 9   I wrote to the church, but Diotrephes, who **loves to have the preeminence [15. philoproteuo]**...among them, does not receive us.

:11   **Beloved [3. agapetos]**, do not imitate what is evil, but what is good. He who does good is of God, but he who does evil has not seen God.

❏ Jude

: 2   Mercy, peace, and **love [2. agape]**...be multiplied to you.

: 3	**Beloved [3. agapetos]**, while I was very diligent to write to you concerning our common salvation, I found it necessary to write to you exhorting you to contend earnestly for the faith which was once for all delivered to the saints.
:12	These are spots in your...**love feasts [2. agape]**, while they feast with you without fear, serving *only* themselves. *They are* clouds without water, carried about by the winds; late autumn trees without fruit, twice dead, pulled up by the roots;
:17	But you, **beloved [3. agapetos]**, remember the words which were spoken before by the apostles of our Lord Jesus Christ:
:20	But you, **beloved [3. agapetos]**, building yourselves up on your most holy faith, praying in the Holy Spirit,
:21	keep yourselves in the **love [2. agape]**...of God, looking for the mercy of our Lord Jesus Christ unto eternal life.

❑ Revelation

1: 5	and from Jesus Christ, the faithful witness, the firstborn from the dead, and the ruler over the kings of the earth. To Him who **loved [1. agapao]**...us and washed us from our sins in His own blood,
2: 4	"Nevertheless I have *this* against you, that you have left your first...**love [2. agape]**."
2:19	"I know your works, **love [2. agape]**, service, faith, and your patience; and *as* for your works, the last *are* more than the first."
3: 9	"Indeed I will make *those* of the synagogue of Satan, who say they are Jews and are not, but lie—indeed I will make them come and worship before your feet, and to know that I have **loved [1. agapao]**...you."
3:19	"As many as I...**love [14. phileo]**, I rebuke and chasten. Therefore be zealous and repent."
12:11	"And they overcame him by the blood of the Lamb and by the word of their testimony, and they did not **love [1. agapao]**...their lives to the death."
20: 9	They went up on the breadth of the earth and surrounded the camp of the saints and the **beloved [1. agapao]**...city. And fire came down from God out of heaven and devoured them.
22:15	But outside *are* dogs and sorcerers and sexually immoral and murderers and idolaters, and whoever **loves [14. phileo]**...and practices a lie.

PART II:

The Word
LOVE
Throughout
The Old Testament

The LORD has appeared of old to me, saying: "Yes, I have loved you with an everlasting love; Therefore with lovingkindness I have drawn you."

—Jeremiah 31:3

The Old Testament Word Sections

Every Hebrew Word
Translated as any Form of
The Word LOVE

I will love You, O LORD, my strength.

—Psalm 18:1

OT WORD 1. 'AGAB

To Desire Sensually

עָגַב *aw-gav´*. Verb. *To lust*. Strong's: H 5689.

To have inappropriate affection, to desire sensually, to lust. As a participle, *those being desired*, i.e., *lovers*.

The LORD warns Judah of Babylon's impending invasion, trying to convince them to repent and change. Without God-given strength, wisdom, and ingenuity, they won't be able to withstand the assault. Because Judah has turned away from Him and does not seek His help, the foreign army will invade and prevail.

In previous chapters, He lamented the idolatry (spiritual adultery) of the people (Jer. 2:5, 11–13, 27–28), the sexually immoral practices associated with idol worship (Jer. 3:2), and the seeking of military alliances with the pagan nations Egypt and Assyria. (Jer. 2:18, 36–37)

Comparing Judah to an unfaithful wife (Jer. 3:1,20), the LORD declares that the "lovers" (military allies) she has chosen will prove as disloyal and treacherous on the day of her calamity as she has been to Him.

⋮≡ TRANSLATION TALLY

lusted	6	time(s)	Eze 23:5, 7, 9, 12, 16, 20
lovers	1	"	See *You and God*

YOU AND GOD

Jeremiah
4:30 (27–30)

LOVE THROUGHOUT THE OLD TESTAMENT / 123

OT WORD 2. ʿAGABIM

Carnal Desire

עֲגָבִים *ag-aw-veem´*. From *ʿagab* (Word 1). Noun (plural). (Sensuous) *loves*. Strong's: H 5690 *ʿegeb*.

Ezekiel was a temple priest and a prophet. He was among the captives carried away from Jerusalem to Babylon after the first siege in 597 BC. (2 Kings 24:10–16) While in exile, Ezekiel prophesied Jerusalem's second siege and consequent destruction that took place in 586 BC. (Ezek. 24:1–2,15–27; 2 Kings 24:20)

The LORD shared with Ezekiel that the Jewish community in exile was not convinced his prophetic ministry was genuine. They gossiped about him and came with insincere affection, responding to his ministry as to an entertaining singer. They set their hearts on their personal interests and gain, not on obeying his words.

The LORD assured Ezekiel that the people would recognize him as a true prophet when news of the fall of Jerusalem reached them. Hopefully then, they would take his messages to heart and seal their faith with obedience.

In Ezekiel 33:31, *ʿagabim* means *love, devotion*, not necessarily sincere. (Cp. Mark 7:6) In Ezekiel 33:32, it means "a song *of loves*," i.e., a *love* song or a *very lovely* song.

≣ TRANSLATION TALLY

much love	1	time	See *You and God*
very lovely	1	"	" " "

 **YOU AND GOD**

Ezekiel
   33:31, 32 (30–33)

OT WORD 3. 'AHAB

Love is a Force

אָהַב *aw-hav'.* Verb. *To love.* Strong's: H 157 *'aheb.*

The primary Old Testament verb "to love," *'ahab* is like the English word "love" in that it is used in many ways. *'Ahab* expresses *affection, longing,* and *desire* of all kinds.

'Ahab communicates *God's love* for Israel, Jerusalem, righteousness, and justice. It refers to *human love* for God, His name, and spiritual things like His Word, righteousness, wisdom, knowledge, and understanding. It speaks of love between the sexes; unselfish love for neighbors, strangers, masters, and friends; and loving such things as food, drink, farming, and sleep.

The first mention of love in the Bible is when God asks Abraham to sacrifice his "only son Isaac, whom you love." (Gen. 22:2) The first mention of love in the New Testament is the Father speaking of *His* beloved Son, in whom He was well pleased, who became the sacrifice for mankind's sin. (Matt. 3:17)

The Passionate Love of God

'Ahab describes the intense love of the One who so desired a family made in His image that He created mankind. He did not make a race of robots but gave us freedom of choice like His. We have the liberty to choose love as the most authentic way to live, loving God and others voluntarily and not from a pre-programmed reflex.

'Ahab is more than mere liking but breathes with the primitive force and passion of God the Father—the original Personality—whose bigger-than-life, jealous love for Israel allowed no breach of loyalty. (Ex. 20:2–6) God wasn't jealous for His own sake but to protect those He loved from the corrupting worship of false deities.

This ancient Hebrew verb brought life to the colorless *agapao/agape* word family used to translate *'ahab* in the Greek version of the Old Testament, the Septuagint. The vocabulary of the Septuagint, in turn, shaped the language of the New Testament. (See NT Words 1 and 2.)

The Great Commandment

'Ahab is the word used in the great commandment of the law.

> "You shall **love** [3. *'ahab*]...the LORD your God with all your heart, with all your soul, and with all your strength." —Deuteronomy 6:5

OT WORD 3. 'AHAB

God called His people to love Him with all their being. They were to know Him, speak of Him, obey Him, adhere to Him, and worship Him. Motivated by their love for Him, they were to serve and obey in righteousness and holiness. (Deu. 10:12, 11:13,22, 30:16)

God promised to bless to a thousand generations *those who love Him and keep His commandments!* (Ex. 20:6, Deut. 5:10, 7:9) *Loving obedience* is still the desired response to the blessings He bestows by grace. We can't *earn* blessings by obedience, but we can demonstrate our love for God. (Cp. John 14:15–17, 21, 23; l John 5:2–3; 2 John :6)

TRANSLATION TALLY

beloved	2	time(s)	2Sa 1:23, Neh 13:26
friend	4	"	2Ch 20:7, Pro 18:24, 27:6, Isa 41:8
friends	8	"	2Sa 19:6, Est 5:10, 14, 6:13, Pro 14:20, Jer 20:4, 6, Zec 13:6
love	90	"	See *You and God*
love, dearly	1	"	Hos 4:18
love, in	1	"	1Ki 11:2
love, made	1	"	Hos 9:1
loved	46	"	See *You and God*
loved one(s)	2	"	Ps 38:11, 88:18
lovers	16	"	See *You and God*
loves	36	"	" " "
loving	1	"	Isa 56:10

YOU AND GOD

Genesis	19:34 (33–34)	30:6 (1–6)	18:1 (1–4)
22:2 (1–3)	Deuteronomy	30:16, 20 (15–20)	18:16, 20, 22 (12–22)
24:67 (63–67)	4:37 (34–38)	Joshua	18:28 (28–30)
25:28 (24–28)	5:10 (5–10)	22:5 (4–6)	20:17 (12–17)
27:4, 9, 14 (1–14)	6:5 (4–9)	23:11 (7–11)	2 Samuel
29:18 (15–20)	7:9, 13 (9–15)	Judges	1:23 (21–24)
29:30, 32 (26–32)	10:12, 15, 18, 19, 11:1	5:31 (28–31)	12:24 (21–25)
34:3 (1–4)	(10:12–11:1)	14:16 (15–17)	13:1, 4 (1–4)
37:3, 4 (3–5)	11:13 (13–17)	16:4 (4–6)	13:15 (10–15)
44:20 (18–22)	11:22 (22–24)	16:15 (15–17)	19:6 (4–7)
Exodus	13:3 (1–4)	Ruth	1 Kings
20:6 (1–6)	15:16 (15–17)	4:15 (13–16)	3:3 (1–5)
21:5 (2–6)	19:9 (7–10)	1 Samuel	5:1 (1–5)
Leviticus	21:15, 16 (15–17)	1:5 (2–5)	11:1, 2 (1–6)
19:18 (15–18)	23:5 (3–6)	16:21 (19–23)	2 Chronicles

126 / LOVE THROUGHOUT THE OLD TESTAMENT

11:21 (21–23)
19:2 (1–3)
26:10 (8–10)
Nehemiah
  1:5 (3–6)
  13:26 (23–27)
Esther
  2:17 (15–17)
Job
  19:19 (17–20)
Psalms
  4:2 (1–3)
  5:11 (10–12)
  11:5, 7 (4–7)
  26:8 (6–8)
  31:23 (21–24)
  33:5 (1–5)
  34:12 (11–16)
  37:28 (27–31)
  38:11 (9–12)
  40:16 (15–17)
  45:7 (6–8)
  47:4 (1–4)
  52:3, 4 (1–5)
  69:36 (34–36)
  70:4 (1–5)
  78:68 (67–69)
  87:2 (1–3)
  88:18 (15–18)
  97:10 (10–12)
  99:4 (1–5)
  109:17 (17–19)
  116:1 (1–5)
  119:47, 48 (45–48)
  119:97 (97–100)
  119:113, 119 (113–120)
  119:127 (126–128)
  119:132 (129–133)
  119:140 (138–142)
  119:159 (158–160)
  119:163, 165, 167 (161–168)
  122:6 (6–9)
  145:20 (18–21)
  146:8 (8–10)
Proverbs
  1:22 (20–23)
  3:12 (11–14)
  4:6 (5–9)
  8:17, 21 (12–21)
  8:36 (32–36)
  9:8 (7–9)
  12:1 (1–3)
  13:24 (23–25)
  15:9, 12 (7–12)
  16:13 (12–15)
  17:17, 19 (16–19)
  18:21 (19–22)
  19:8 (6–9)
  20:13 (11–14)
  21:17 (16–18)
  22:11 (9–12)
  29:3 (2–4)
Ecclesiastes
  3:8 (5–8)
  5:10 (10–12)
  9:9 (7–10)
Song of Solomon
  1:3, 4 (2–4)
  1:7 (7–8)
  3:1, 2, 3, 4 (1–5)
Isaiah
  1:23 (21–23)
  43:4 (1–4)
  48:14 (12–15)
  56:6 (6–8)
  56:10 (9–11)
  57:8 (7–9)
  61:8 (6–9)
  66:10 (10–13)
Jeremiah
  2:25 (22–25)
  5:31 (28–31)
  8:2 (1–2)
  14:10 (8–10)
  22:20, 22 (20–22)
  30:14 (11–14)
  31:3 (1–4)
Lamentations
  1:2 (1–2)
  1:19 (18–19)
Ezekiel
  16:33, 36, 37 (30–38)
  23:5, 9 (5–10)
  23:22 (22–24)
Daniel
  9:4 (2–5)
Hosea
  2:5, 7, 10, 12, 13 (4–13)
  3:1 (1–3)
  4:18 (17–19)
  9:1 (8:14–9:2)
  9:10 (10–12)
  10:11 (11–13)
  11:1 (1–4)
  12:7 (6–8)
  14:4 (1–5)
Amos
  4:5 (4–5)
  5:15 (14–15)
Micah
  3:2 (1–2)
Zechariah
  8:17, 19 (14–19)
Malachi
  1:2 (1–3)
  2:11 (10–12)

OT WORD 4. 'AHABAH

Love

אַהֲבָה *ah-ha-vaw´*. From *'ahab* (Word 3). Noun. *Love*. Strong's: H 160.

'Ahabah refers to *affection* and *liking*, much like the root *'ahab* and the English word "love." It signifies (1) the love of the LORD for His people (especially Deut. 7:8, Isa. 63:9, Jer. 31:3, Hos. 11:4, Zeph. 3:17); (2) tender affection between man and wife (Gen. 29:20, Prov. 5:19, Song 2:4, etc.); (3) brotherly love and covenant loyalty (1 Sam. 18:3, 20:17); and (4) human love in general. God's covenant love and faithfulness are usually expressed by *hesed* (Word 11).

☰ TRANSLATION TALLY

love	31 time(s)	See *You and God*	
loved	5 "	" " "	
loves	2 "	" " "	
lovesick (+ *halah*)	2 "	" " "	

YOU AND GOD

Genesis	2 Chronicles	9:1, 6 (1–6)	2:2 (1–3)
29:20 (15–20)	2:11 (11–12)	Song of Solomon	2:33 (31–33)
Deuteronomy	9:8 (5–9)	2:4, 5, 7 (4–7)	31:3 (3–6)
7:8 (6–8)	Psalms	3:5 (1–5)	Hosea
1 Samuel	109:4, 5 (1–5)	3:10 (9–11)	3:1 (1–3)
18:3 (1–4)	Proverbs	5:8 (6–8)	9:15 (15–17)
20:17 (12–17)	5:19 (15–20)	7:6 (4–6)	11:4 (1–4)
2 Samuel	10:12 (11–13)	8:4 (1–4)	Micah
1:26 (24–27)	15:17 (16–18)	8:6, 7 (5–7)	6:8 (6–8)
13:15 (12–16)	17:9 (8–10)	Isaiah	Zephaniah
1 Kings	27:5 (4–6)	63:9 (7–9)	3:17 (14–17)
10:9 (6–10)	Ecclesiastes	Jeremiah	

OT WORD 5. 'AHABIM

Affectionate Love

אֲהָבִים *a-haw-veem´*. From *'ahab* (Word 3). Noun (plural). *Loves.* Strong's: H 158 *'ahab*.

'Ahabim means *loves, affection,* and *delight.* It is used figuratively in a good and bad sense: (1) of a wife, a *"loving doe,"* affectionate and *full of grace;* (2) of foreign nations, *"lovers,"* whom Israel hired for military protection rather than trusting in God.

 Translation Tally

lovers	1	time	See *You and God*
loving	1	"	" " "

You and God

Proverbs
5:19 (15–20)

Hosea
8:9 (8–12)

OT WORD 6. DOD

A Beloved One

דּוֹד *dohd*. Noun. *Loved one.* Strong's: H 1730 *dowd*.

Dod refers to a *loved one*, a *beloved*, an *intimate friend*: (1) specifically in the Song of Solomon, the *beloved* of the Shulamite maiden; (2) in the plural, *love, expressions of love*; (3) the *friend* of the family, a *father's brother* or paternal *uncle*.

≡ TRANSLATION TALLY

beloved	32	time(s)	See *You and God*
beloved ones	1	"	Song 5:1
father's brothers	1	"	Numbers 36:11
kinsman	1	"	Amos 6:10
love	8	"	See *You and God*
uncle	11	"	Lev 10:4, 25:49, 1Sa 10:14, 15, 16, 14:50, 2Ki 24:17, 1Ch 27:32, Est 2:15, Jer 32:7, 9
uncle's	5	"	Lev 20:20, 25:49, Est 2:7, Jer 32:8, 12

YOU AND GOD

Proverbs	2:8, 9, 10, 16, 17	7:9, 10, 11, 12, 13	Ezekiel
7:18 (14–20)	(8–17)	(9–13)	16:8 (8–10)
Song of Solomon	4:10, 16, 5:1 (4:9–5:1)	8:5 (5–7)	23:17 (16–18)
1:2, 4 (2–4)	5:2, 4, 5, 6, 8, 9, 10,	8:14 (11–14)	
1:13, 14, 16, 2:3	16, 6:1, 2, 3	Isaiah	
(1:12–2:3)	(5:2–6:3)	5:1 (1–4)	

OT WORD 7. 'ETNAN

Love for Hire

 *et-nan'*. From *tanah* (*to give presents, hire, pay*). Noun. *Payment.* Strong's: H 868 *'ethnan*.

'Etnan is a *gift*, specifically, the *price* of a prostitute. In the *You and God* text, God judged Jerusalem for hiring (paying the prostitute price of) foreign powers for military protection. Their actions lacked faith in His ability to protect the nation. Jerusalem also engaged in pagan worship (spiritual adultery) with the idol gods of those nations. (Ezekiel 16:36)

:≡ TRANSLATION TALLY

hire	1	time(s)	Deu 23:18
lovers	1	"	See *You and God*
pay	5	"	Isa 23:17, 18, Mic 1:7
payment	3	"	Eze 16:31, 34
reward	1	"	Hos 9:1

📝 YOU AND GOD

Ezekiel
 16:41 (38–42)

OT WORD 8. HABAB

To Cherish

חָבַב *khaw-vav´.* Verb. *To love.* Strong's: H 2245 *chabab.*

Habab means to *cherish* (as *enfolding* to the bosom), to *embrace* with fervent and protective love.

God gave the law of Moses to Israel *in tender love.* As they obeyed its precepts, He blessed them with favor and the protection of His embrace. (Cp. Deut. 7:12–16, 28:1–14) The law was fiery with God's wisdom, righteousness, and glory. But no one could keep it perfectly although the law was the brightest revelation of its day.

Fortunately, the grace and truth which came through Jesus Christ are more glorious than the law. (John 1:17, 2 Cor. 3:7–11) Jesus gave us the gift of *His* perfect righteousness being imputed to our accounts, zeroing out our sin debt. He brought believers into right standing with God, something which could not happen under the law. (Rom. 5:15–21, 2 Cor. 5:21) Those who trust in Jesus become as if they had never sinned and are eligible to be cherished in God's loving and protective embrace. Christ's disciples are to sit at His feet and receive His Words, as Mary did. (Luke 10:38–42)

☰ TRANSLATION TALLY

loves   1   time   See *You and God*

 YOU AND GOD

Deuteronomy
33:3 (1–5)

OT WORD 9. HAMUDOT

Precious

חֲמוּדוֹת *kha-moo-doht´*. From *hamad* (*to desire, delight in*). Noun (plural). *Precious things*. Strong's: H 2530 *chamudoth*.

Hamudot is a *person* or *thing of great value, precious, choice, desirable,* and *highly esteemed.*

Daniel was a *precious treasure* in the sight of the LORD. He cared enough to fast and pray for the restoration of Israel from her Babylonian captivity. In the eyes of the LORD, he was *precious*. God blessed him with prophecies concerning the Messiah to come.

 TRANSLATION TALLY

choice	1	time(s)	Gen 27:15
greatly beloved	3	"	See *You and God*
pleasant	1	"	Dan 10:3
pleasant things	1	"	Dan 11:38
precious	2	"	2Ch 20:25, Ezr 8:27
precious things	1	"	Dan 11:43

✍ YOU AND GOD

Daniel
9:23 (20–24)   10:11 (10–14)   10:19 (17–19)

OT WORD 10. HASHAQ

To Cling to in Love

חָשַׁק *khaw-shak´*. Verb. *To be attached to*. Strong's: H 2836 *chashaq*.

Hashaq means *to connect* or *join together*. Concerning the heart, it refers to *being attached to* in love, *clinging to* with delight or desire, and *setting one's affection on*. Regarding the tabernacle, it denotes *to join with bands*.

God's love for His people is a *bond*, an *attachment*, an *adhering*, a *clinging* with emotional ties. (Deut. 7:7) As He has *set his love on* us, we are *to attach* ourselves to Him, *bond* to Him, *cling* to Him, and *adhere* to Him in every circumstance. (Ps. 91:14) When we remain attached to Him, His love elevates us to victory over every obstacle.

Just as an airplane carries passengers over the mountains to their destination, God's love conveys us on eagle's wings over the difficulties we face. But we must cling to Him, stay in the plane, and not parachute out if we hit turbulence.

:≡ TRANSLATION TALLY

bands, have	2	time(s)	Ex 27:17, 38:17
band, made	1	"	Ex 38:28
delighted	1	"	Deu 10:15
desire	1	"	Deu 21:11
desired	2	"	1Ki 9:19, 2Ch 8:6
longs	1	"	Gen 34:8
love, set	2	"	See *You and God*
lovingly *delivered*	1	"	" " "

 YOU AND GOD

Deuteronomy	Psalms	Isaiah
7:7 (6–8)	91:14 (14–16)	38:17 (15–19)

134 / LOVE THROUGHOUT THE OLD TESTAMENT

OT WORD 11. HESED

Covenant Love

חֶסֶד *heh-´sed*. From *hasad* (*to be kind*). Noun. *Lovingkindness*. Strong's: H 2617 *chesed*.

Hesed is the great Hebrew word for the *loyal love, steadfast lovingkindness,* and *mercy* of God toward men, and the *kindness* and *mercy* of man to man.

Hesed refers to *covenant love*. It describes the *love* and *loyalty* God expected in response to His covenant with Israel. The LORD promised to keep "covenant and *mercy [hesed]* for a thousand generations with those who love Him and keep His commandments." (Deut. 7:9, cp. Ex. 20:6, Deut. 7:12, 1 Kings 8:23, Neh. 1:5, 9:32, Ps. 89:28, 33–34, 106:45, Dan. 9:4, Luke 1:72) He expected no less from His people.

The Most Solemn, Sacred Agreements

Covenants are the most solemn, sacred agreements known to man. In the Bible, parties to a covenant pledged to show *hesed* to each other—even if helping their covenant partner required their life! Covenant love (*hesed*) consisted of *kindness, mercy, love, loyalty,* and *faithfulness*.

Covenants were made between God and individuals such as Abraham and David, God and the nation of Israel, husbands and wives, masters and servants, and kings and vassals. (See Gen. 20:13, 21:23, 24:12, 14, 32:10, 39:21, Josh. 2:12, 1 Sam. 20:8, 14, 15)

God pledged to Abraham and his seed/Seed to be a God to them and to bless them. (Gen. 12:1–3, 17:1–7, 22:16–18, Gal. 3:16–29) In return, God's people were to show *hesed* toward Him—*devotion, faithfulness,* and *steadfast love.* (Jer. 2:2, Hos. 6:4) They were also to show *hesed* to each other—*kindness, mercy,* and brotherly *love*. (Hos. 6:6, Mic. 6:8, Zech. 7:9–10, Matt. 9:13, 12:7, 5:7, Luke 6:36)

The Steadfast Love of God

At times, Israel's faithful devotion to God (*hesed*) vanished like a morning cloud as the day warmed. (Hos. 6:4) They broke the covenant they pledged to keep and departed from the exclusive worship of Yahweh. But God is the great I AM. (Ex. 3:14, 34:6–7) Though men vacillated, He remained faithful to the covenant, having given His Word which cannot change. God's *hesed* is *loyal love*. When men's unfaithfulness made the mercy of God undeserved, His *hesed* took on the character of *grace* as He sought to draw Israel back to Himself. (Lam. 3:22–23, Jer. 3:1)

Anyone who has experienced God's *hesed,* been touched by *grace* in the face of failure, and known His *merciful lovingkindness* will ever be praising Him! In the Book of Psalms alone, God's *hesed* is extolled 124 times. He is worthy of praise!

When Solomon dedicated the temple, the choirs and musicians sang, "For He is good, for His *mercy [hesed]* endures forever!" As they did, the glory cloud of God's presence filled the temple, and the priests became unable to minister. (2 Chron. 5:13–14, see also 7:3, 6, 20:21–22)

God's *hesed* is called "great" (Num. 14:19, 1 Kings 3:6, Neh. 13:22, Ps. 103:11, 145:8, Joel 2:13), "marvelous" (Ps. 17:7, 31:21), "abounding" (Ex. 34:6, Ps. 103:8, Isa. 63:7b), "precious" (Ps. 36:7), "everlasting" (Ps. 100:5, 103:17, 136:1, 2, [etc.], Isa. 54:8), and "sure" (Isa. 55:3).

The New Covenant

God made the New Covenant with those who believe Jesus is the Christ. (Matt. 26:28, Heb. 8:10–12, 9:15, 12:24) Faith in Jesus introduces us to God's *grace, steadfast covenant love, faithfulness,* and *mercy.* In Christ, we experience the *hesed* of God as His incredible *grace.*

TRANSLATION TALLY

faithfulness	1	time(s)	Hos 6:4
favor	4	"	Est 2:9, 17, Job 10:12, Dan 1:9
good deeds	1	"	Neh 13:14
goodness	10	"	Ex 34:6, 2Ch 32:32, 35:26, Ps 33:5, 52:1, 107:8, 15, 21, 31, Pro 20:6
kindly	5	"	Gen 24:49, 47:29, Jos 2:14, Ruth 1:8, 1Sa 20:8
kindness	35	"	Gen 20:13, 21:23, 24:12, 24:14, etc.
loveliness	1	"	Isa 40:6
lovingkindness	29	"	See *You and God*
lovingkindnesses	4	"	" " "
loyalty	2	"	2Sa 3:8, 16:17
merciful	4	"	1Ki 20:31, Ps 59:10, Pro 11:17, Isa 57:1
merciful kindness	2	"	Ps 117:2, 119:76
mercy	135	"	Gen 19:19, 24:27, 39:21, etc.
mercies	11	"	Gen 32:10, 2Ch 6:42, Ps 31:16, 44:26, 89:1, 106:7, 45, 119:41, Isa 55:3, Lam 3:22, 32

✎ YOU AND GOD

Psalms	69:16 (14–18)	138:2 (1–3)	16:5 (1–5)
17:7 (6–9)	88:11 (9–12)	143:8 (7–10)	31:3 (1–4)
25:6 (4–7)	89:33 (30–37)	144:2 (1–2)	32:18 (16–19)
26:3 (1–3)	89:49 (46–49)	Proverbs	Hosea
36:7, 10 (5–10)	92:2 (1–4)	20:28 (27–29)	2:19 (16–20)
40:10, 11 (6–11)	103:4 (1–5)	Isaiah	Jonah
42:8 (6–8)	107:43 (40–43)	40:6 (6–8)	4:2 (1–5)
48:9 (8–10)	119:88 (85–88)	63:7 (7–10)	
51:1 (1–4)	119:149 (147–149)	Jeremiah	
63:3 (1–5)	119:159 (157–160)	9:24 (23–24)	

OT WORD 12. MAHMAD

Desirable

מַחְמָד *makh-mawd´*. Noun. From *hamad* (*to desire, delight in*). *Desire, desirable thing*. Strong's: H 4261 *machmad*.

Mahmad is *something greatly desired, pleasant,* and *precious*. It is a *delight*, such as a spouse (Ezek. 24:16), a child (Hos. 9:16), or a treasured possession (Joel 3:5). In the *You and God* text, the Shulamite maiden describes her beloved as "altogether... *lovely (mahmad).*" She sees in him all that is pleasant, desirable, and delightful.

☰ TRANSLATION TALLY

darlings	1	time(s)	Hos 9:16
desire	3	"	Eze 24:16, 21, 25
lovely	1	"	See *You and God*
pleasant	1	"	1Ki 20:6
pleasant things	2	"	Isa 64:11, Lam 1:10
pleasing	1	"	Lam 2:4
prized possessions (+ *tobim*)	1	"	Joel 3:5
precious	1	"	2Ch 36:19
valuables	2	"	Lam 1:11, Hos 9:6

 YOU AND GOD

Song of Solomon
5:16

138 / LOVE THROUGHOUT THE OLD TESTAMENT

OT WORD 13. NA'AH

To Be Beautiful

נָאָה *naw-aw´.* Verb. *To be attractive.* Strong's: H 4998.

Na'ah refers to *loveliness* based on the suitability, compatibility, and harmony of parts in a whole. When features agree pleasantly, are right for each other, and fit well together, they are *becoming* or *beautiful.* (See Word 14.)

For example, holiness fits well with and beautifies God's house, being suitable and harmonious.

> Your testimonies are very sure;
> Holiness **adorns [na'ah]**…Your house,
> O LORD, forever. —Psalms 93:5

Holiness of life is a complementary response to God's majesty and unchanging testimonies, which bear witness to His steadfast love and care.

Likewise, the feet of the messenger who proclaims, "Your God reigns!" are called *beautiful (fitting, appropriate, right)* on the mountains of Moriah, where Jerusalem is situated. (Isa. 52:7) Isaiah prophesied that one day a messenger would arrive with the good news that Babylon, Israel's captor, had been overthrown and Jerusalem redeemed.

> How **beautiful [na'ah]**…upon the mountains
> Are the feet of him who brings good news,
> Who proclaims peace,
> Who brings glad tidings of good things,
> Who proclaims salvation,
> Who says to Zion, "Your God reigns!" —Isaiah 52:7

In the prophetic picture, the runner is near and ascending the mountains surrounding Jerusalem. The harmony of his liberating message and its fast-approaching delivery makes his feet beautiful. Even more beautiful are the feet of the swift messengers who publish better news—of Satan's overthrow by the triumph of Jesus Christ! (Cp. Rom. 10:15–16)

In the Song of Solomon 1:10 (see *You and God*), the fair cheeks and neck of the Shulamite maiden enhance her earrings and necklaces as much as her ornaments become and adorn her face. Each complements and sets off the other, which is the nature of true beauty.

:≡ TRANSLATION TALLY

adorns	1	time	Ps 93:5
beautiful, be	1	"	Isa 52:7
lovely, be	1	"	See *You and God*

 YOU AND GOD

Song of Solomon
 1:10 (7–10)

OT WORD 14. NA'VEH

Lovely

נָאוֶה *naw-veh´.* From *na'ah* (Word 13). Adjective. *Lovely.* Strong's: H 5000.

Na'veh describes the beauty of composite parts that are well-arranged and suitable to each other, yielding a harmony of the whole (see Word 13). It is used in a negative sense of things incompatible and incongruous. (Prov. 17:7, 19:10, 26:1) *Na'veh* twice describes how fitting and beautiful it is for the righteous to rejoice and praise God. (Ps. 33:1, 147:1) Righteousness and praise perfectly complement each other.

> Rejoice in the LORD, O you righteous!
> For praise from the upright is…*beautiful [na'veh].* —Psalm 33:1

In the *You and God* texts, *na'veh* depicts the beauty of a lovely woman whose features are attractive because of the harmony of their arrangement.

 Translation Tally

beautiful	2	time(s)	Ps 33:1, 147:1
becoming	1	"	Pro 17:7
fitting	2	"	Pro 19:10, 26:1
lovely	5	"	See *You and God*

📖 YOU AND GOD

Song of Solomon	4:3 (2–4)	Jeremiah
1:5 (5–6)	6:4 (4–7)	6:2 (1–3)
2:14 (13–15)		

OT WORD 15. 'OHABIM

Sensual Love

אֲהָבִים *o-haw-veem´*. From *'ahab* (Word 3). Noun (plural). *(Sensual) loves, affections.* Strong's: H 159 *'ohab*.

Scripture includes this account of the adulterous affair to impart wisdom to the simple-minded. It gives the young man knowledge and discretion, warns him of impending spiritual death, and delivers him from the "immoral woman...the seductress who flatters with her words" (Prov. 2:16, 7:5). Her "house is the way to hell, descending to the chambers of death." (Prov. 7:27)

Beware of those who have no sacred regard for the marriage covenant, whose idea of "love" is limited to the physical. God's Word compares the one seduced by an immoral person to an ox led to slaughter, a fool to public correction in the stocks, a bird flitting into a deathtrap, and an unwary soul wandering into a den of demons scheming to possess his body with insatiable lust.

☰ TRANSLATION TALLY

love   1   time   See *You and God*

 YOU AND GOD

Proverbs
7:18 (10–27)

142 / LOVE THROUGHOUT THE OLD TESTAMENT

OT WORD 16. RAHAM

To Have Compassion

רָחַם *raw-kham´*. Verb. *To have compassion.* Strong's: H 7355 *racham*.

Raham expresses *having compassion* for those with whom one shares a familial or unifying bond. It speaks of the special mercy a parent has for a child. (Isa. 49:15) It refers to God's compassion for His own. (Jer. 31:20, Ps. 103:13, Hos. 2:23) Contrast that with the lack of compassion shown by foreign conquerors, who have no mercy on those they defeat. (Jer. 6:23, 50:42)

Particularly touching is the use of *raham* in Hosea 14:3, "In You the fatherless...*finds mercy [raham].*" Those who can't relate to an earthly father find in God a firm, appropriate love and compassion never before experienced. He is the original and best Father. The psalmist said, "When my father and my mother forsake me, then the LORD will take care of me." (Psalm 27:10)

In Isaiah 54:8 and 10, *raham* occurs in parallel with *hesed* (see Word 11). Each word amplifies the meaning of the other. God says that with everlasting *hesed* He will *raham*, or have compassion on, His people.

David sang Psalm 18 on the day he was delivered from Saul. It begins, "I will *love [raham]* You, O LORD, my strength!" His use of *raham* (instead of the more general *'ahab*, Word 3) suggests he loved the LORD as a Father with whom he had a close-knit spiritual bond. The heat and pressure of years of persecution forged those ties while David depended prayerfully on God alone for protection from the hand of Saul.

≔ TRANSLATION TALLY

compassion (on), have	9	time(s)	Ex 33:19, Deu 13:17, 30:3, 1Ki 8:50, 2Ki 13:23, Isa 49:15, Jer 12:15, Mic 7:19
compassion, show	1	"	Lam 3:32
-Ruhamah	2	"	Hos 1:6, 8
love	1	"	See *You and God*
merciful	1	"	Ps 116:5
mercy	1	"	Hab 3:2
mercy, finds	1	"	Hos 14:3
mercy, have	26	"	Ps 102:13, Pro 28:13, Isa 9:17, 14:1, 27:11, 30:18, 49:10, 13, 54:8, 10, 55:7, 60:10, Jer 6:23, 13:14, 21:7, 30:18, 31:20, 33:26,

42:12, Eze 39:25, Hos 1:6,7, 2:4, 23, Zec 1:12, 10:6

Mercy is shown	1	time(s)	Hos 2:1
mercy, obtained	1	"	Hos 2:23
mercy, show	1	"	Jer 50:42
pities	2	"	Ps 103:13
pity, have	1	"	Isa 13:18
surely	1	"	Jer 31:20

 **YOU AND GOD**

Psalms
18:1 (1–3)

OT WORD 17. RA'YAH

A Female Friend

 rah-yaw´. Feminine of *rea'* (Word 18). Noun. *A female friend.* Strong's: H 7474.

Ra'yah means a *female companion.* Specifically, in the Song of Solomon, *ra'yah* refers to the Shulamite maiden, the beloved bride. Her beloved calls her "my *love.*"

TRANSLATION TALLY

love　　　　　　　　9　times　　　See *You and God*

YOU AND GOD

Song of Solomon 　　2:10, 13 (8–13)　　5:2 (2–6)
　1:9, 15, 2:2 (1:9–2:3)　4:1, 7 (1–8)　　　6:4 (4–7)

OT WORD 18. REA'
A Neighbor

רֵעַ *ray'-ah*. From *ra'ah* (in the sense *to associate with*). Noun. *Neighbor.* Strong's: H 7453.

The primary Hebrew word for "neighbor," *rea'* encompasses a spectrum of relationships, from the impersonal to the intimate. In general, *rea'* refers to one's *fellow* (Gen. 11:3), a *neighbor* (Deut. 19:14), a *fellow* Israelite (Ex. 2:13), an *associate* in some relation (2 Sam. 2:16, "opponent"), or in the remotest sense, simply *another*. (Gen. 15:10, Ruth 3:14) In the nearest applications, *rea'* signifies a *companion* (Judges 7:13), a *friend* (Job 2:11), or even a *husband* or *lover*. (See *You and God*.)

In the Ten Commandments, *rea'* was applied broadly to a man's dealings with his neighbor, that is, anyone and everyone, whoever he may be. (Ex. 20:16, 17)

"You shall not bear false witness against [lie about] your…**neighbor [rea']**."
—Exodus 20:16

The Rabbinic Interpretation

Some ancient rabbis interpreted the word differently in the familiar Leviticus 19:18.

"You shall not take vengeance, nor bear any grudge against the children of your people, but you shall **love** [3. **'ahab**] your **neighbor [rea']**…as yourself: I am the LORD."

The parallelism between "children of your people" and "neighbor" was understood to narrow the meaning of *rea'* to a fellow Israelite. In support of a broader interpretation (applying the word "neighbor" to anyone and everyone), Leviticus 19:34 commanded the children of Israel to love every foreigner and alien as though he were an Israelite.

"The stranger [alien] who dwells among you shall be to you as one born among you, and you shall **love [3. 'ahab]**…him as yourself; for you were strangers in the land of Egypt: I am the LORD your God."

Who Is My Neighbor?

In Jesus' day, despite the extensive and general Old Testament use of *rea'*, a debate continued over the correct interpretation of "neighbor" in Leviticus 19:18. Some favored a definition for "neighbor" restricted to fellow Israelites and proselytes to

Judaism. This view was implied by the lawyer's famous question to Jesus, "And who is my neighbor?" It prompted Jesus to teach the parable of the Good Samaritan. (Luke 10:29–37)

Jesus recast the question from "Who is my neighbor?" to "...which of these *was neighbor* to him who fell among thieves?" (Luke 10:36) Which of these *acted like a neighbor*? Which of these showed love? Jesus removed the "religious" cloak from those who preferred to love (and help) only those of their race, religion, and culture, exposing the hardness of many hearts.

The Second Commandment

Jesus interpreted "neighbor" to include not only one's religious and racial "neighbor" but all humanity (regardless of race, religion, culture, or origin)—and even one's enemies! (Matt. 5:43–48) Jesus required the righteousness of His disciples to *exceed* that of the scribes, lawyers, and Pharisees. (Matt. 5:20)

:≡ TRANSLATION TALLY

another ('s)	23	time(s)	Gen 11:3, 7, 31:49, 43:33, Ex 18:16, etc.
brother	1	"	Deu 24:10
companion	8	"	Ex 2:13, 32:27, Jud 7:13, 14, 22, 1Ch 27:33, Job 30:29, Isa 34:14
companions	2	"	Job 35:4, Zec 3:8
companions'	1	"	Ps 122:8
friend	28	"	Gen 38:12, 20, Ex 33:11, Deu 13:6, etc.
friends	16	"	1Sa 30:26, 1Ki 16:11, Job 2:11, 12:4, etc.
husband	1	"	Jer 3:20
lover	1	"	See *You and God*
lovers	1	"	" " "
neighbor('s)	97	"	Ex 11:2a, 20:16, 17, 21:14, 22:7, etc.
neighbors	2	"	Ps 28:3, Eze 22:12
opponent	1	"	2Sa 2:16
opponent's	1	"	2Sa 2:16
other	4	"	Gen 15:10, Ex 18:7, 21:18, Ruth 4:7

YOU AND GOD

Jeremiah
3:1 (1–4)

Hosea
3:1 (1–3)

OT WORD 19. SANE'

To Hate

שָׂנֵא *saw-nay'*. Verb. *To hate*. Strong's: H 8130.

Sane' is a significant word despite its negative definition. It is used with a range of meanings that extends from *malicious hatred* with the intent to harm (Gen. 37:4, 8ff, Deut. 19:11); to *rejection, dislike,* or *disregard* (Deut. 24:3, Prov. 13:24); to being *loved less* in comparison. (See *You and God*.)

The word is used for human and divine hatred. Human hatred originated in the fall of Adam and was manifested by Cain against his brother Abel. Its frequent occurrence exposes sinful man's separation from God, who is love. (Gen. 4:8–9, 6:5, 13, 1 John 4:8,16, 3:14–15, 2:9–11) God has hatred, too—for sin. Why? Because it destroys the lives of those He loves. (Deut. 12:31, Prov. 6:16–19)

⋮≡ TRANSLATION TALLY

detests	3	time(s)	Deu 22:13, 16, 24:3
enemies	4	"	Ex 1:10, 2Sa 19:6, 2Ch 1:11, Est 9:16
enemy	2	"	Pro 25:21, 27:6
hate	68	"	Gen 24:60, 26:27, Ex 20:5, etc.
hated	35	"	Gen 37:4, 5, 8, Deu 4:42, etc.
hateful	1	"	Pro 30:23
haters	1	"	Ps 81:15
hates	23	"	Ex 23:5, Deu 7:10, 16:22, etc.
hating	1	"	Ex 18:21
thoroughly hated	1	"	Jud 15:2
unloved	6	"	See *You and God*

YOU AND GOD

Genesis
29:31, 33 (31–35)

Deuteronomy
21:15, 16, 17 (15–17)

OT WORD 20. SHAPPIR

Elegant

שַׁפִּיר  shap-peer´. Aramaic, adjective. *Beautiful, fair, elegant.* Strong's: H 8209 *shappiyr*.

Shappir described the elegant leaves of the tree seen in a vision by Nebuchadnezzar, king of Babylon. Beautiful, rich green leaves and abundant fruit symbolized the security and prosperity of his reign. (Compare Ps. 1:3 and Jer. 17:8.)

⁝≡ TRANSLATION TALLY

lovely   2   times   See *You and God*

📖 YOU AND GOD

Daniel
    4:12 (9–12)
    4:21 (19–22)

OT WORD 21. TOB

Good

תוֹב *tohv*. From *tob* (*to be, make,* or *do good, well*). Adjective, noun. *Good.* Strong's: H 2896 *towb*.

Tob is the chief Hebrew word for *good*. It occurs approximately 550 times in the Old Testament with wide-ranging meanings. It is used for (1) that which is *good, ethical, kind,* or *beneficial* in God's or men's moral nature (Deut. 12:28, 2 Chron. 10:7, Ps. 34:8, 73:1, 107:1); (2) of the spiritual and material *blessings* of God, *good things, prosperity, bounty, security* (Num. 10:29, Deut. 23:6, Ps. 25:13, Isa. 52:7, Jer. 18:10); (3) of that which is *pleasant* or *beautiful* to the senses (Gen. 3:6, 24:16, Josh. 7:21); (4) *agreeable* and *enjoyable* to the mind (Gen. 20:15, 1 Sam. 3:18); (5) *excellent* of its type (Gen. 1:4, etc., 31, 27:9, Ex. 3:8, 1 Sam. 8:16, 2 Chron. 3:5); (6) *abundant* in quantity (Gen. 15:15); (7) *rich* or *valuable* (Deut. 28:12, Prov. 31:18, Joel 3:5); (8) *becoming* or *appropriate* to a situation or circumstance (2 Sam. 17:7, Eccl. 7:11); etc.

≡ TRANSLATION TALLY

agreeable	1	time(s)	Zec 11:12
beautiful	12	"	Gen 6:2, 24:16, 26:7, Ex 2:2, Deu 6:10, 8:12, Jos 7:21, 2Sa 11:2, Est 1:11, 2:2, 3, 7
benefit	1	"	Ps 106:5
best	10	"	Num 36:6, Deu 23:16, Jud 10:15, 1Sa 8:14, 15:9, 2Ki 10:3, Est 2:9, Song 7:9, Eze 31:16, Mic 7:4
better	76	"	Gen 29:19, Ex 14:12, Num 14:3, Jud 8:2, 9:2, 11:25, 15:2, etc.
bountiful	1	"	Pro 22:9
bounty	1	"	Hos 10:1
cheerful	1	"	Zec 8:19
choice	1	"	Gen 27:9
encourage	2	"	1Ki 22:13, 2Ch 18:12
encouragement	2	"	1Ki 22:13, 2Ch 18:12
favor	2	"	1Sa 2:26, 29:6
feast	1	"	1Sa 25:8
fine	4	"	2Ch 3:5, 8, Ezr 8:27, Lam 4:1
finest	1	"	1Sa 8:16
glad	3	"	1Ki 8:66, 2Ch 7:10, Est 5:9
good (men)	339	"	

			Gen 1:4, 10, 12, 18, 21, 25, 31, 2:9, 12, 17, 18, 3:5, 6, 22, 15:15, etc.
good deeds	1	"	Neh 6:19
good- [looking]	3	"	1Sa 16:12, 1Ki 1:6, Dan 1:4
goodness	14	"	2Sa 7:28, 1Ki 8:66, 1Ch 17:26, 2Ch 6:41, Ps 16:2, 21:3, 23:6, 65:11, 68:10, 107:9, Pro 2:20, Ecc 6:3, 6, Jer 33:9
goods	2	"	Deu 28:11, Ecc 5:11
graciously	1	"	Hos 14:2
handsome (more)	2	"	1Sa 9:2
high	1	"	Pro 3:4
holi- [day]	3	"	Est 8:17, 9:19, 22
joyful	1	"	Ecc 7:14
kind	1	"	2Ch 10:7
kindly	2	"	2Ki 25:28, Jer 52:32
kindness	1	"	2Sa 2:6
loveliest	1	"	See *You and God*
lovely	1	"	" " "
loving	1	"	" " "
merry	6	"	Jud 16:25, 1Sa 25:36, 2Sa 13:28, Est 1:10, Pro 15:15, Ecc 9:7
more	1	"	2Sa 18:3
pleasant	3	"	Deu 3:25, 2Ki 2:19, Ecc 11:7
please	9	"	Gen 16:6, 20:15, Jud 19:24, 2Sa 3:36, Est 8:5, 8, 9:13, Ecc 7:26
pleasure	2	"	Job 21:25, Ecc 2:1
precious	3	"	2Ki 20:13, Ps 133:2, Isa 39:2
prized	1	"	Joel 3:5
prosperity	8	"	Deu 23:6, 1Ki 10:7, Ezr 9:12, Job 36:11, Ps 25:13, Ecc 7:14, Lam 3:17, Zec 1:17
ready	1	"	Isa 41:7
seductive [+ hen]	1	"	Nah 3:4
smooth words	1	"	Jer 12:6
sweet	1	"	Jer 6:20
wealth	1	"	Job 21:13
well (very)	17	"	Jud 9:16, 1Sa 9:10, 19:4, 20:7, 24:18, 1Ki 2:18, 18:24, 2Ch 12:12, Ps 119:65, 128:2, Pro 13:2, Ecc 8:12, 13, Isa 3:10, Jer 15:11, 22:15, 16
well-being	2	"	Neh 2:10, Lam 3:38
well-off	1	"	Jer 44:17
wish	1	"	Gen 19:8

 YOU AND GOD

Numbers
24:5 (5–7)

1 Kings
20:3 (1–3)

Proverbs
22:1 (1–4)

OT WORD 22. YADID

A Beloved

יָדִיד *yaw-deed'*. Adjective, also as noun. *Beloved, lovely.* Strong's: H 3039 *yediyd*.

Yadid refers to one *greatly loved*, a *beloved* or *friend* of God or man. It signifies the *beloved* of the LORD five times. (Deut. 33:12, Ps. 127:2, etc.) Once, *yadid* describes the tabernacle of the LORD as being *lovely* and *pleasant.* (Ps. 84:1) Twice, Isaiah calls Jehovah his *Well-beloved*. (Isa. 5:1)

We see the plural of *yadid* in the heading of Psalm 45, meaning a "song of *love*" or a "song of *beloveds*." It was probably styled after songs sung at weddings to the bride and groom. This psalm depicts the glory, majesty, strength, and joy of the royal Bridegroom, Jesus the Messiah, as He prepares to receive His bride, the Church.

⋮☰ TRANSLATION TALLY

beloved	5 time(s)	See *You and God*	
love	1 "	" " "	
lovely	1 "	" " "	
well-beloved	2 "	" " "	

YOU AND GOD

Deuteronomy
  33:12 (12)
Psalms
  45:Heading

60:5 (3–5)
84:1 (1–4)
108:6 (3–6)
127:2 (1–2)

Isaiah
  5:1 (1–4)
Jeremiah
  11:15 (13–17)

OT WORD 23. YAPHEH

Beautiful

יָפֶה *yaw-feh´.* From *yaphah (to be beautiful).* Adjective. *Beautiful.* Strong's: H 3303.

Yapheh describes that which is *beautiful* or *lovely.* Most frequently, it characterizes (1) a *beautiful* woman (Gen. 12:11, 29:17, etc.); (2) sometimes a *handsome* man (Gen. 39:6, 1 Sam. 17:42, 2 Sam. 14:25); (3) in other cases, cattle (Gen. 41:2,4,18); (4) trees (Jer. 11:16, Ezek. 31:3,9); (5) a singing voice (Ezek. 33:32); (6) Jerusalem (Ps. 48:2); (7) everything in its time (Eccl. 3:11); and (8) enjoying the fruits of one's labor (Eccl. 5:18). The beauty may be internal as well as external (cp. Song 4:7). Hadassah (Esther) is described as *yapheh* in combination with *toar*, meaning beautiful or lovely in appearance and form (Esther 2:7).

≣ TRANSLATION TALLY

beautiful	11	time(s)	Gen 12:11, 14, 29:17, Deu 21:11, 1Sa 25:3, 2Sa 14:27, Job 42:15, Ps 48:2, Ecc 3:11, Song 6:4, Eze 31:9
bright	1	"	1Sa 16:12
fair (one)	9	"	Song 1:15, 2:10, 13, 4:1, 7, 6:10, Amos 8:13
fairest	3	"	Song 1:8, 5:9, 6:1
fine	4	"	Gen 41:2, 4, 18, Eze 31:3
fitting	1	"	Ecc 5:18
good-	1	"	1Sa 17:42
good looks [+*adam*]	1	"	2Sa 14:25
handsome	2	"	Gen 39:6, Song 1:16
lovely	5	"	See *You and God*
lovely [+*toar*]	1	"	Est 2:7, See *You and God*
pleasant	1	"	Eze 33:32

 YOU AND GOD

2 Samuel
  13:1 (1–4)
1 Kings
  1:3, 4 (1–4)

Esther
  2:7 (7–8)
Proverbs
  11:22 (20–23)

Jeremiah
  11:16 (13–17)

OT WORD 24. YEDIDUT

Dearly Beloved

יְדִדוּת  y'dee-doot'. From *yadid* (Word 22). Noun. *Dearly beloved*. Strong's: H 3033 *yediduwth*.

Yedidut properly means *love* or *affection*. Here it is used for the object of love, a *beloved one*, a *dearly beloved*, a *darling*.

In the text below, the LORD tells Jeremiah He is withdrawing His protection from Judah because she has rejected His efforts to restore her. He describes her as the "*yedidut* of My soul," a phrase that shows how much His heart longs for her return (cp. Hos. 11:8). Yet, despite God's love and steadfast faithfulness, Judah has spurned Him as a wife who leaves her husband for another. She has persisted in worshiping idols.

≔ TRANSLATION TALLY

dearly beloved	1 time	See *You and God*

🕮 YOU AND GOD

Jeremiah
12:7 (6–9)

"Hear, O Israel: The LORD our God, the LORD is one! You shall love the LORD your God with all your heart, with all your soul, and with all your strength. And these words which I command you today shall be in your heart. You shall teach them diligently to your children, and shall talk of them when you sit in your house, when you walk by the way, when you lie down, and when you rise up."

—Deuteronomy 6:4–7

The Old Testament Verse Concordance

Every Use of
Any Form of
The Word
LOVE

Including...
*Beloved, Beloved's, Love, Loved,
Loveliest, Loveliness, Lovely, Lover,
Lovers, Loves, Lovesick, Loving,
Lovingkindness, Lovingkindnesses,
Lovingly, Unloved*

"You shall not take vengeance, nor bear any grudge against the children of your people, but you shall love your neighbor as yourself: I am the LORD."

—Leviticus 19:18

OLD TESTAMENT VERSE CONCORDANCE

For the meaning and usage of the Hebrew words in bold print, refer to the corresponding Old Testament Word Sections. The New Testament Verse Concordance begins on page 99.

The following Scriptures are taken from the New King James Version®. Copyright © 1982 by Thomas Nelson. Used by permission. All rights reserved.

❏ Genesis

22: 2	Then He said, "Take now your son, your only *son* Isaac, whom you…**love** [3. 'ahab], and go to the land of Moriah, and offer him there as a burnt offering on one of the mountains of which I shall tell you."
24:67	Then Isaac brought her into his mother Sarah's tent; and he took Rebekah and she became his wife, and he **loved** [3. 'ahab]…her. So Isaac was comforted after his mother's *death*.
25:28	And Isaac **loved** [3. 'ahab]…Esau because he ate *of his* game, but Rebekah **loved** [3. 'ahab]…Jacob.
27: 4	"And make me savory food, such as I…**love** [3. 'ahab], and bring *it* to me that I may eat, that my soul may bless you before I die."
27: 9	"Go now to the flock and bring me from there two choice kids of the goats, and I will make savory food from them for your father, such as he…**loves** [3. 'ahab]."
27:14	And he went and got *them* and brought *them* to his mother, and his mother made savory food, such as his father…**loved** [3. 'ahab].
29:18	Now Jacob **loved** [3. 'ahab]…Rachel; so he said, "I will serve you seven years for Rachel your younger daughter."
29:20	So Jacob served seven years for Rachel, and they seemed *only* a few days to him because of the **love** [4. 'ahabah]…he had for her.
29:30	Then *Jacob* also went in to Rachel, and he also **loved** [3. 'ahab]…Rachel more than Leah. And he served with Laban still another seven years.
29:31	When the LORD saw that Leah *was*…**unloved** [19. sane'], He opened her womb; but Rachel *was* barren.

LOVE THROUGHOUT THE OLD TESTAMENT / 159

29:32	So Leah conceived and bore a son, and she called his name Reuben; for she said, "The LORD has surely looked on my affliction. Now therefore, my husband will **love** [3. **'ahab**]...me."
29:33	Then she conceived again and bore a son, and said, "Because the LORD has heard that I *am*...**unloved** [19. **sane'**], He has therefore given me this *son* also." And she called his name Simeon.
34: 3	His soul was strongly attracted to Dinah the daughter of Jacob, and he **loved** [3. **'ahab**]...the young woman and spoke kindly to the young woman.
37: 3	Now Israel **loved** [3. **'ahab**]...Joseph more than all his children, because he *was* the son of his old age. Also he made him a tunic of *many* colors.
37: 4	But when his brothers saw that their father **loved** [3. **'ahab**]...him more than all his brothers, they hated him and could not speak peaceably to him.
44:20	"And we said to my lord, 'We have a father, an old man, and a child of *his* old age, *who is* young; his brother is dead, and he alone is left of his mother's children, and his father **loves** [3. **'ahab**]...him.'"

❏ Exodus

20: 6	"but showing mercy to thousands, to those who **love** [3. **'ahab**]...Me and keep My commandments."
21: 5	"But if the servant plainly says, 'I **love** [3. **'ahab**]...my master, my wife, and my children; I will not go out free,'"

❏ Leviticus

19:18	"You shall not take vengeance, nor bear any grudge against the children of your people, but you shall **love** [3. **'ahab**]...your neighbor as yourself: I am the LORD."
19:34	"The stranger who dwells among you shall be to you as one born among you, and you shall **love** [3. **'ahab**]...him as yourself; for you were strangers in the land of Egypt: I *am* the LORD your God."

❏ Numbers

24: 5	"How **lovely** [21. **tob**]...are your tents, O Jacob! Your dwellings, O Israel!"

❏ Deuteronomy

4:37	"And because He **loved** [3. 'ahab]...your fathers, therefore He chose their descendants after them; and He brought you out of Egypt with His Presence, with His mighty power,"
5:10	"but showing mercy to thousands, to those who **love** [3. 'ahab]...Me and keep My commandments."
6: 5	"You shall **love** [3. 'ahab]...the LORD your God with all your heart, with all your soul, and with all your strength."
7: 7	"The LORD did not **set** His **love** [10. hashaq]...on you nor choose you because you were more in number than any other people, for you were the least of all peoples;"
7: 8	"But because the LORD **loves** [4. 'ahabah]...you, and because He would keep the oath which He swore to your fathers, the LORD has brought you out with a mighty hand, and redeemed you from the house of bondage, from the hand of Pharaoh king of Egypt."
7: 9	"Therefore know that the LORD your God, He *is* God, the faithful God who keeps covenant and mercy for a thousand generations with those who **love** [3. 'ahab]...Him and keep His commandments;"
7:13	"And He will **love** [3. 'ahab]...you and bless you and multiply you; He will also bless the fruit of your womb and the fruit of your land, your grain and your new wine and your oil, the increase of your cattle and the offspring of your flock, in the land of which He swore to your fathers to give you."
10:12	"And now, Israel, what does the LORD your God require of you, but to fear the LORD your God, to walk in all His ways and to **love** [3. 'ahab]...Him, to serve the LORD your God with all your heart and with all your soul,"
10:15	"The LORD delighted only in your fathers, to **love** [3. 'ahab]...them; and He chose their descendants after them, you above all peoples, as *it is* this day."
10:18	"He administers justice for the fatherless and the widow, and **loves** [3. 'ahab]...the stranger, giving him food and clothing."
10:19	"Therefore **love** [3. 'ahab]...the stranger, for you were strangers in the land of Egypt."
11: 1	"Therefore you shall **love** [3. 'ahab]...the LORD your God, and keep His charge, His statutes, His judgments, and His commandments always."
11:13	"And it shall be that if you earnestly obey My commandments which I command you today, to **love** [3. 'ahab]...the LORD your God and serve Him with all your heart and with all your soul,"

LOVE THROUGHOUT THE OLD TESTAMENT

11:22	"For if you carefully keep all these commandments which I command you to do—to **love** [3. 'ahab]...the LORD your God, to walk in all His ways, and to hold fast to Him—"
13: 3	"you shall not listen to the words of that prophet or that dreamer of dreams, for the LORD your God is testing you to know whether you **love** [3. 'ahab]...the LORD your God with all your heart and with all your soul."
15:16	"And if it happens that he says to you, 'I will not go away from you,' because he **loves** [3. 'ahab]...you and your house, since he prospers with you,"
19: 9	"and if you keep all these commandments and do them, which I command you today, to **love** [3. 'ahab]...the LORD your God and to walk always in His ways, then you shall add three more cities for yourself besides these three,"
21:15	"If a man has two wives, one **loved** [3. 'ahab]...and the other...**unloved** [19. sane'], and they have borne him children, *both* the **loved** [3. 'ahab]...and the...**unloved** [19. sane'], and *if* the firstborn son is of her who is...**unloved** [19. sane'],"
21:16	"then it shall be, on the day he bequeaths his possessions to his sons, *that* he must not bestow firstborn status on the son of the **loved** [3. 'ahab]...wife in preference to the son of the...**unloved** [19. sane'], the *true* firstborn."
21:17	"But he shall acknowledge the son of the **unloved** [19. sane']...wife *as* the firstborn by giving him a double portion of all that he has, for he *is* the beginning of his strength; the right of the firstborn *is* his."
23: 5	"Nevertheless the LORD your God would not listen to Balaam, but the LORD your God turned the curse into a blessing for you, because the LORD your God **loves** [3. 'ahab]...you."
30: 6	"And the LORD your God will circumcise your heart and the heart of your descendants, to **love** [3. 'ahab]...the LORD your God with all your heart and with all your soul, that you may live."
30:16	"in that I command you today to **love** [3. 'ahab]...the LORD your God, to walk in His ways, and to keep His commandments, His statutes, and His judgments, that you may live and multiply; and the LORD your God will bless you in the land which you go to possess."
30:20	"that you may **love** [3. 'ahab]...the LORD your God, that you may obey His voice, and that you may cling to Him, for He *is* your life and the length of your days; and that you may dwell in the land which the LORD swore to your fathers, to Abraham, Isaac, and Jacob, to give them."
33: 3	"Yes, He **loves** [8. habab]...the people; All His saints *are* in Your hand; They sit down at Your feet; *Everyone* receives Your words."

33:12   Of Benjamin he said:

    "The **beloved** [22. yadid]...of the LORD shall dwell in safety by Him,
    Who shelters him all the day long;
    And he shall dwell between His shoulders."

❏ Joshua

22: 5   "But take careful heed to do the commandment and the law which Moses the servant of the LORD commanded you, to **love** [3. 'ahab]...the LORD your God, to walk in all His ways, to keep His commandments, to hold fast to Him, and to serve Him with all your heart and with all your soul."

23:11   "Therefore take careful heed to yourselves, that you **love** [3. 'ahab]...the LORD your God."

❏ Judges

5:31   "Thus let all Your enemies perish, O LORD!
    But let those who **love** [3. 'ahab]...Him be like the sun
    When it comes out in full strength."

So the land had rest for forty years.

14:16   Then Samson's wife wept on him, and said, "You only hate me! You do not **love** [3. 'ahab]...me! You have posed a riddle to the sons of my people, but you have not explained it to me." And he said to her, "Look, I have not explained it to my father or my mother; so should I explain it to you?"

16: 4   Afterward it happened that he **loved** [3. 'ahab]...a woman in the Valley of Sorek, whose name was Delilah.

16:15   Then she said to him, "How can you say, 'I **love** [3. 'ahab]...you,' when your heart is not with me? You have mocked me these three times, and have not told me where your great strength lies."

❏ Ruth

4:15   "And may he be to you a restorer of life and a nourisher of your old age; for your daughter-in-law, who **loves** [3. 'ahab]...you, who is better to you than seven sons, has borne him."

❏ 1 Samuel

1: 5   But to Hannah he would give a double portion, for he **loved** [3. 'ahab]...Hannah, although the LORD had closed her womb.

16:21	So David came to Saul and stood before him. And he **loved** [3. 'ahab]...him greatly, and he became his armorbearer.
18: 1	Now when he had finished speaking to Saul, the soul of Jonathan was knit to the soul of David, and Jonathan **loved** [3. 'ahab]...him as his own soul.
18: 3	Then Jonathan and David made a covenant, because he **loved** [4. 'ahabah]...him as his own soul.
18:16	But all Israel and Judah **loved** [3. 'ahab]...David, because he went out and came in before them.
18:20	Now Michal, Saul's daughter, **loved** [3. 'ahab]...David. And they told Saul, and the thing pleased him.
18:22	And Saul commanded his servants, "Communicate with David secretly, and say, 'Look, the king has delight in you, and all his servants **love** [3. 'ahab]... you. Now therefore, become the king's son-in-law.' "
18:28	Thus Saul saw and knew that the LORD *was* with David, and *that* Michal, Saul's daughter, **loved** [3. 'ahab]...him;
20:17	Now Jonathan again caused David to vow, because he **loved** [4. 'ahabah]...him; for he **loved** [3. 'ahab]...him as he **loved** [4. 'ahabah]...his own soul.

❑ 2 Samuel

1:23	"Saul and Jonathan *were* **beloved** [3. 'ahab]...and pleasant in their lives,
	  And in their death they were not divided;
	  They were swifter than eagles,
	  They were stronger than lions."

1:26	"I am distressed for you, my brother Jonathan;
	  You have been very pleasant to me;
	  Your **love** [4. 'ahabah]...to me was wonderful,
	  Surpassing the **love** [4. 'ahabah]...of women."

12:24	Then David comforted Bathsheba his wife, and went in to her and lay with her. So she bore a son, and he called his name Solomon. Now the LORD **loved** [3. 'ahab]...him,
13: 1	After this Absalom the son of David had a **lovely** [23. yapheh]...sister, whose name *was* Tamar; and Amnon the son of David **loved** [3. 'ahab]...her.
13: 4	And he said to him, "Why *are* you, the king's son, becoming thinner day after day? Will you not tell me?" Amnon said to him, "I **love** [3. 'ahab]... Tamar, my brother Absalom's sister."

13:15   Then Amnon hated her exceedingly, so that the hatred with which he hated her *was* greater than the **love** [4. **'ahabah**]...with which he had **loved** [3. **'ahab**]...her. And Amnon said to her, "Arise, be gone!"

19: 6   "in that you **love** [3. **'ahab**]...your enemies and hate your friends. For you have declared today that you regard neither princes nor servants; for today I perceive that if Absalom had lived and all of us had died today, then it would have pleased you well."

❏ 1 Kings

1: 3   So they sought for a **lovely** [23. **yapheh**]...young woman throughout all the territory of Israel, and found Abishag the Shunammite, and brought her to the king.

1: 4   The young woman *was* very...**lovely** [23. **yapheh**]; and she cared for the king, and served him; but the king did not know her.

3: 3   And Solomon **loved** [3. **'ahab**]...the LORD, walking in the statutes of his father David, except that he sacrificed and burned incense at the high places.

5: 1   Now Hiram king of Tyre sent his servants to Solomon, because he heard that they had anointed him king in place of his father, for Hiram had always **loved** [3. **'ahab**]...David.

10: 9   "Blessed be the LORD your God, who delighted in you, setting you on the throne of Israel! Because the LORD has **loved** [4. **'ahabah**]...Israel forever, therefore He made you king, to do justice and righteousness."

11: 1   But King Solomon **loved** [3. **'ahab**]...many foreign women, as well as the daughter of Pharaoh: women of the Moabites, Ammonites, Edomites, Sidonians, *and* Hittites—

11: 2   from the nations of whom the LORD had said to the children of Israel, "You shall not intermarry with them, nor they with you. Surely they will turn away your hearts after their gods." Solomon clung to these in...**love** [4. **'ahabah**].

20: 3   " 'Your silver and your gold *are* mine; your **loveliest** [21. **tob**]...wives and children are mine.' "

❏ 2 Chronicles

2:11   Then Hiram king of Tyre answered in writing, which he sent to Solomon:

         Because the LORD **loves** [4. **'ahabah**]...His people, He has made you king over them.

9: 8   "Blessed be the LORD your God, who delighted in you, setting you on His throne *to be* king for the LORD your God! Because your God has **loved** [4.

	'ahabah]...Israel, to establish them forever, therefore He made you king over them, to do justice and righteousness."
11:21	Now Rehoboam **loved** [**3. 'ahab**]...Maachah the granddaughter of Absalom more than all his wives and his concubines; for he took eighteen wives and sixty concubines, and begot twenty-eight sons and sixty daughters.
19: 2	And Jehu the son of Hanani the seer went out to meet him, and said to King Jehoshaphat, "Should you help the wicked and **love** [**3. 'ahab**]...those who hate the LORD? Therefore the wrath of the LORD *is* upon you."
26:10	Also he built towers in the desert. He dug many wells, for he had much livestock, both in the lowlands and in the plains; *he also had* farmers and vinedressers in the mountains and in Carmel, for he **loved** [**3. 'ahab**]...the soil.

❏ Nehemiah

1: 5	And I said: "I pray, LORD God of heaven, O great and awesome God, *You* who keep *Your* covenant and mercy with those who **love** [**3. 'ahab**]...You and observe Your commandments,"
13:26	"Did not Solomon king of Israel sin by these things? Yet among many nations there was no king like him, who was **beloved** [**3. 'ahab**]...of his God; and God made him king over all Israel. Nevertheless pagan women caused even him to sin."

❏ Esther

2: 7	And *Mordecai* had brought up Hadassah, that *is*, Esther, his uncle's daughter, for she had neither father nor mother. The young woman *was* **lovely** [**23. yapheh**]...and beautiful. When her father and mother died, Mordecai took her as his own daughter.
2:17	The king **loved** [**3. 'ahab**]...Esther more than all the *other* women, and she obtained grace and favor in his sight more than all the virgins; so he set the royal crown upon her head and made her queen instead of Vashti.

❏ Job

19:19	"All my close friends abhor me, And those whom I **love** [**3. 'ahab**]...have turned against me."

❏ Psalms

4: 2	How long, O you sons of men, *Will you turn* my glory to shame?

	How long will you **love** [3. 'ahab]…worthlessness *And* seek falsehood? Selah
5:11	But let all those rejoice who put their trust in You; Let them ever shout for joy, because You defend them; Let those also who **love** [3. 'ahab]…Your name Be joyful in You.
11: 5	The LORD tests the righteous, But the wicked and the one who **loves** [3. 'ahab]…violence His soul hates.
11: 7	For the LORD *is* righteous, He **loves** [3. 'ahab]…righteousness; His countenance beholds the upright.
17: 7	Show Your marvelous **lovingkindness** [11. hesed]…by Your right hand, O You who save those who trust *in You* From those who rise up *against them.*
18: 1	I will **love** [16. raham]…You, O LORD, my strength.
25: 6	Remember, O LORD, Your tender mercies and Your… **lovingkindnesses** [11. hesed], For they *are* from of old.
26: 3	For Your **lovingkindness** [11. hesed]…*is* before my eyes, And I have walked in Your truth.
26: 8	LORD, I have **loved** [3. 'ahab]…the habitation of Your house, And the place where Your glory dwells.
31:23	Oh, **love** [3. 'ahab]…the LORD, all you His saints! *For* the LORD preserves the faithful, And fully repays the proud person.
33: 5	He **loves** [3. 'ahab]…righteousness and justice; The earth is full of the goodness of the LORD.
34:12	Who *is* the man *who* desires life, And **loves** [3. 'ahab]…*many* days, that he may see good?
36: 7	How precious *is* Your…**lovingkindness** [11. hesed], O God! Therefore the children of men put their trust under the shadow of Your wings.
36:10	Oh, continue Your **lovingkindness** [11. hesed]…to those who know You, And Your righteousness to the upright in heart.
37:28	For the LORD **loves** [3. 'ahab]…justice, And does not forsake His saints;

	They are preserved forever, But the descendants of the wicked shall be cut off.
38:11	My **loved ones** [3. 'ahab]...and my friends stand aloof from my plague, And my relatives stand afar off.
40:10	I have not hidden Your righteousness within my heart; I have declared Your faithfulness and Your salvation; I have not concealed Your **lovingkindness** [11. hesed]...and Your truth From the great assembly.
40:11	Do not withhold Your tender mercies from me, O LORD; Let Your **lovingkindness** [11. hesed]...and Your truth continually preserve me.
40:16	Let all those who seek You rejoice and be glad in You; Let such as **love** [3. 'ahab]...Your salvation say continually, "The LORD be magnified!"
42: 8	The LORD will command His **lovingkindness** [11. hesed]...in the daytime, And in the night His song *shall be* with me— A prayer to the God of my life.
45: Heading	To the Chief Musician. Set to "The Lilies." A Contemplation of the sons of Korah. A Song of...**Love** [22. yadid].
45: 7	You **love** [3. 'ahab]...righteousness and hate wickedness; Therefore God, Your God, has anointed You With the oil of gladness more than Your companions.
47: 4	He will choose our inheritance for us, The excellence of Jacob whom He...**loves** [3. 'ahab]. Selah
48: 9	We have thought, O God, on Your...**lovingkindness** [11. hesed], In the midst of Your temple.
51: 1	Have mercy upon me, O God, According to Your...**lovingkindness** [11. hesed]; According to the multitude of Your tender mercies, Blot out my transgressions.
52: 3	You **love** [3. 'ahab]...evil more than good, Lying rather than speaking righteousness. Selah
52: 4	You **love** [3. 'ahab]...all devouring words, *You* deceitful tongue.
60: 5	That Your **beloved** [22. yadid]...may be delivered, Save *with* Your right hand, and hear me.

63: 3	Because Your **lovingkindness** [11. hesed]...*is* better than life, My lips shall praise You.
69:16	Hear me, O LORD, for Your **lovingkindness** [11. hesed]...*is* good; Turn to me according to the multitude of Your tender mercies.
69:36	Also, the descendants of His servants shall inherit it, And those who **love** [3. 'ahab]...His name shall dwell in it.
70: 4	Let all those who seek You rejoice and be glad in You; And let those who **love** [3. 'ahab]...Your salvation say continually, "Let God be magnified!"
78:68	But chose the tribe of Judah, Mount Zion which He...**loved** [3. 'ahab].
84: 1	How **lovely** [22. yadid]...*is* Your tabernacle, O LORD of hosts!
87: 2	The LORD **loves** [3. 'ahab]...the gates of Zion More than all the dwellings of Jacob.
88:11	Shall Your **lovingkindness** [11. hesed]...be declared in the grave? *Or* Your faithfulness in the place of destruction?
88:18	**Loved one** [3. 'ahab]...and friend You have put far from me, *And* my acquaintances into darkness.
89:33	"Nevertheless My **lovingkindness** [11. hesed]...I will not utterly take from him, Nor allow My faithfulness to fail."
89:49	Lord, where *are* Your former...**lovingkindnesses** [11. hesed], *Which* You swore to David in Your truth?
91:14	"Because he has **set** his **love** [10. hashaq]...upon Me, therefore I will deliver him; I will set him on high, because he has known My name."
92: 2	To declare Your **lovingkindness** [11. hesed]...in the morning, And Your faithfulness every night,
97:10	You who **love** [3. 'ahab]...the LORD, hate evil! He preserves the souls of His saints; He delivers them out of the hand of the wicked.
99: 4	The King's strength also **loves** [3. 'ahab]...justice; You have established equity; You have executed justice and righteousness in Jacob.
103: 4	Who redeems your life from destruction, Who crowns you with **lovingkindness** [11. hesed]...and tender mercies,

107:43	Whoever *is* wise will observe these *things*, And they will understand the **lovingkindness** [11. hesed]...of the LORD.
108: 6	That Your **beloved** [22. yadid]...may be delivered, Save *with* Your right hand, and hear me.
109: 4	In return for my **love** [4. 'ahabah]...they are my accusers, But I *give myself to* prayer.
109: 5	Thus they have rewarded me evil for good, And hatred for my...**love** [4. 'ahabah].
109:17	As he **loved** [3. 'ahab]...cursing, so let it come to him; As he did not delight in blessing, so let it be far from him.
116: 1	I **love** [3. 'ahab]...the LORD, because He has heard My voice *and* my supplications.
119:47	And I will delight myself in Your commandments, Which I...**love** [3. 'ahab].
119:48	My hands also I will lift up to Your commandments, Which I...**love** [3. 'ahab], And I will meditate on Your statutes.
119:88	Revive me according to Your...**lovingkindness** [11. hesed], So that I may keep the testimony of Your mouth.
119:97	Oh, how I **love** [3. 'ahab]...Your law! It *is* my meditation all the day.
119:113	I hate the double-minded, But I **love** [3. 'ahab]...Your law.
119:119	You put away all the wicked of the earth *like* dross; Therefore I **love** [3. 'ahab]...Your testimonies.
119:127	Therefore I **love** [3. 'ahab]...Your commandments More than gold, yes, than fine gold!
119:132	Look upon me and be merciful to me, As Your custom *is* toward those who **love** [3. 'ahab]...Your name.
119:140	Your word *is* very pure; Therefore Your servant **loves** [3. 'ahab]...it.
119:149	Hear my voice according to Your...**lovingkindness** [11. hesed]; O LORD, revive me according to Your justice.
119:159	Consider how I **love** [3. 'ahab]...Your precepts; Revive me, O LORD, according to Your...**lovingkindness** [11. hesed].
119:163	I hate and abhor lying, *But* I **love** [3. 'ahab]...Your law.

119:165	Great peace have those who **love** [3. 'ahab]...Your law, And nothing causes them to stumble.
119:167	My soul keeps Your testimonies, And I **love** [3. 'ahab]...them exceedingly.
122: 6	Pray for the peace of Jerusalem: "May they prosper who **love** [3. 'ahab]...you."
127: 2	*It is* vain for you to rise up early, To sit up late, To eat the bread of sorrows; *For* so He gives His **beloved** [22. yadid]...sleep.
138: 2	I will worship toward Your holy temple, And praise Your name For Your **lovingkindness** [11. hesed]...and Your truth; For You have magnified Your word above all Your name.
143: 8	Cause me to hear Your **lovingkindness** [11. hesed]...in the morning, For in You do I trust; Cause me to know the way in which I should walk, For I lift up my soul to You.
144: 2	My **lovingkindness** [11. hesed]...and my fortress, My high tower and my deliverer, My shield and *the One* in whom I take refuge, Who subdues my people under me.
145:20	The LORD preserves all who **love** [3. 'ahab]...Him, But all the wicked He will destroy.
146: 8	The LORD opens *the eyes of* the blind; The LORD raises those who are bowed down; The LORD **loves** [3. 'ahab]...the righteous.

❑ Proverbs

1:22	"How long, you simple ones, will you **love** [3. 'ahab]...simplicity? For scorners delight in their scorning, And fools hate knowledge."
3:12	For whom the LORD **loves** [3. 'ahab]...He corrects, Just as a father the son *in whom* he delights.
4: 6	Do not forsake her, and she will preserve you; **Love** [3. 'ahab]...her, and she will keep you.
5:19	*As a* **loving** [5. 'ahabim]...deer and a graceful doe, Let her breasts satisfy you at all times; And always be enraptured with her...**love** [4. 'ahabah].

7:18	"Come, let us take our fill of **love** [6. dod]...until morning; Let us delight ourselves with...**love** [15. 'ohabim]."
8:17	"I **love** [3. 'ahab]...those who **love** [3. 'ahab]...me, And those who seek me diligently will find me."
8:21	"That I may cause those who **love** [3. 'ahab]...me to inherit wealth, That I may fill their treasuries."
8:36	"But he who sins against me wrongs his own soul; All those who hate me **love** [3. 'ahab]...death."
9: 8	"Do not correct a scoffer, lest he hate you; Rebuke a wise *man,* and he will **love** [3. 'ahab]...you."
10:12	Hatred stirs up strife, But **love** [4. 'ahabah]...covers all sins.
11:22	*As* a ring of gold in a swine's snout, *So is* a **lovely** [23. yapheh]...woman who lacks discretion.
12: 1	Whoever **loves** [3. 'ahab]...instruction **loves** [3. 'ahab]... knowledge, But he who hates correction *is* stupid.
13:24	He who spares his rod hates his son, But he who **loves** [3. 'ahab]...him disciplines him promptly.
15: 9	The way of the wicked *is* an abomination to the LORD, But He **loves** [3. 'ahab]...him who follows righteousness.
15:12	A scoffer does not **love** [3. 'ahab]...one who corrects him, Nor will he go to the wise.
15:17	Better *is* a dinner of herbs where **love** [4. 'ahabah]...is, Than a fatted calf with hatred.
16:13	Righteous lips *are* the delight of kings, And they **love** [3. 'ahab]...him who speaks *what is* right.
17: 9	He who covers a transgression seeks...**love** [4. 'ahabah], But he who repeats a matter separates friends.
17:17	A friend **loves** [3. 'ahab]...at all times, And a brother is born for adversity.
17:19	He who **loves** [3. 'ahab]...transgression **loves** [3. 'ahab]...strife, And he who exalts his gate seeks destruction.
18:21	Death and life *are* in the power of the tongue, And those who **love** [3. 'ahab]...it will eat its fruit.
19: 8	He who gets wisdom **loves** [3. 'ahab]...his own soul; He who keeps understanding will find good.

20:13	Do not **love** [**3. 'ahab**]...sleep, lest you come to poverty; Open your eyes, *and* you will be satisfied with bread.
20:28	Mercy and truth preserve the king, And by **lovingkindness** [**11. hesed**]...he upholds his throne.
21:17	He who **loves** [**3. 'ahab**]...pleasure *will be* a poor man; He who **loves** [**3. 'ahab**]...wine and oil will not be rich.
22: 1	A *good* name is to be chosen rather than great riches, **Loving** [**21. tob**]...favor rather than silver and gold.
22:11	He who **loves** [**3. 'ahab**]...purity of heart *And has* grace on his lips, The king *will be* his friend.
27: 5	Open rebuke *is* better Than **love** [**4. 'ahabah**]...carefully concealed.
29: 3	Whoever **loves** [**3. 'ahab**]...wisdom makes his father rejoice, But a companion of harlots wastes *his* wealth.

❏ Ecclesiastes

3: 8	A time to...**love** [**3. 'ahab**], And a time to hate; A time of war, And a time of peace.
5:10	He who **loves** [**3. 'ahab**]...silver will not be satisfied with silver; Nor he who **loves** [**3. 'ahab**]...abundance, with increase. This also *is* vanity.
9: 1	For I considered all this in my heart, so that I could declare it all: that the righteous and the wise and their works *are* in the hand of God. People know neither **love** [**4. 'ahabah**]...nor hatred *by* anything *they see* before them.
9: 6	Also their...**love** [**4. 'ahabah**], their hatred, and their envy have now perished; Nevermore will they have a share In anything done under the sun.
9: 9	Live joyfully with the wife whom you **love** [**3. 'ahab**]...all the days of your vain life which He has given you under the sun, all your days of vanity; for that *is* your portion in life, and in the labor which you perform under the sun.

❏ Song of Solomon

1: 2	Let him kiss me with the kisses of his mouth— For your **love** [**6. dod**]...*is* better than wine.

Song of Solomon

1: 3	Because of the fragrance of your good ointments, Your name *is* ointment poured forth; Therefore the virgins **love** [3. 'ahab]...you.
1: 4	Draw me away! We will run after you. The king has brought me into his chambers. We will be glad and rejoice in you. We will remember your **love** [6. dod]...more than wine. Rightly do they **love** [3. 'ahab]...you.
1: 5	I *am* dark, but...**lovely** [14. na'veh], O daughters of Jerusalem, Like the tents of Kedar, Like the curtains of Solomon.
1: 7	Tell me, O you whom I...**love** [3. 'ahab], Where you feed *your flock,* Where you make *it* rest at noon. For why should I be as one who veils herself By the flocks of your companions?
1: 9	I have compared you, my...**love** [17. ra'yah], To my filly among Pharaoh's chariots.
1:10	Your cheeks are **lovely** [13. na'ah]...with ornaments, Your neck with chains *of gold.*
1:13	A bundle of myrrh *is* my **beloved** [6. dod]...to me, That lies all night between my breasts.
1:14	My **beloved** [6. dod]...*is* to me a cluster of henna *blooms* In the vineyards of En Gedi.
1:15	Behold, you *are* fair, my...**love** [17. ra'yah]! Behold, you *are* fair! You *have* dove's eyes.
1:16	Behold, you *are* handsome, my...**beloved** [6. dod]! Yes, pleasant! Also our bed *is* green.
2: 2	Like a lily among thorns, So *is* my **love** [17. ra'yah]...among the daughters.
2: 3	Like an apple tree among the trees of the woods, So *is* my **beloved** [6. dod]...among the sons. I sat down in his shade with great delight, And his fruit *was* sweet to my taste.
2: 4	He brought me to the banqueting house, And his banner over me *was*...**love** [4. 'ahabah].

174 / LOVE THROUGHOUT THE OLD TESTAMENT

2: 5	Sustain me with cakes of raisins, Refresh me with apples, For I *am* **lovesick** [4. 'ahabah].
2: 7	I charge you, O daughters of Jerusalem, By the gazelles or by the does of the field, Do not stir up nor awaken **love** [4. 'ahabah]... Until it pleases.
2: 8	The voice of my...**beloved** [6. dod]! Behold, he comes Leaping upon the mountains, Skipping upon the hills.
2: 9	My **beloved** [6. dod]...is like a gazelle or a young stag. Behold, he stands behind our wall; He is looking through the windows, Gazing through the lattice.
2:10	My **beloved** [6. dod]...spoke, and said to me: "Rise up, my...**love** [17. ra'yah], my fair one, And come away."
2:13	The fig tree puts forth her green figs, And the vines *with* the tender grapes Give a good smell. "Rise up, my **love** [17. ra'yah], my fair one, And come away!"
2:14	"O my dove, in the clefts of the rock, In the secret *places* of the cliff, Let me see your face, Let me hear your voice; For your voice *is* sweet, And your face *is*...**lovely** [14. na'veh]."
2:16	My **beloved** [6. dod]...*is* mine, and I *am* his. He feeds *his flock* among the lilies.
2:17	Until the day breaks And the shadows flee away, Turn, my **beloved** [6. dod], And be like a gazelle Or a young stag Upon the mountains of Bether.
3: 1	By night on my bed I sought the one I...**love** [3. 'ahab]; I sought him, but I did not find him.
3: 2	"I will rise now," *I said*, "And go about the city; In the streets and in the squares

	I will seek the one I…**love** [3. 'ahab]."
	I sought him, but I did not find him.
3: 3	The watchmen who go about the city found me;
	I said,
	"Have you seen the one I…**love** [3. 'ahab]?"
3: 4	Scarcely had I passed by them,
	When I found the one I…**love** [3. 'ahab].
	I held him and would not let him go,
	Until I had brought him to the house of my mother,
	And into the chamber of her who conceived me.
3: 5	I charge you, O daughters of Jerusalem,
	By the gazelles or by the does of the field,
	Do not stir up nor awaken **love** [4. 'ahabah]…
	Until it pleases.
3:10	He made its pillars of silver,
	Its support *of* gold,
	Its seat *of* purple,
	Its interior paved *with* **love** [4. 'ahabah]…
	By the daughters of Jerusalem.
4: 1	Behold, you *are* fair, my…**love** [17. ra'yah]!
	Behold, you *are* fair!
	You *have* dove's eyes behind your veil.
	Your hair *is* like a flock of goats,
	Going down from Mount Gilead.
4: 3	Your lips *are* like a strand of scarlet,
	And your mouth is…**lovely** [14. na'veh].
	Your temples behind your veil
	Are like a piece of pomegranate.
4: 7	You *are* all fair, my…**love** [17. ra'yah],
	And *there is* no spot in you.
4:10	How fair is your…**love** [6. dod],
	My sister, *my* spouse!
	How much better than wine is your…**love** [6. dod],
	And the scent of your perfumes
	Than all spices!
4:16	Awake, O north *wind,*
	And come, O south!
	Blow upon my garden,
	That its spices may flow out.
	Let my **beloved** [6. dod]…come to his garden
	And eat its pleasant fruits.

5: 1	I have come to my garden, my sister, *my* spouse; I have gathered my myrrh with my spice; I have eaten my honeycomb with my honey; I have drunk my wine with my milk. Eat, O friends! Drink, yes, drink deeply, O…**beloved ones [6. dod]**!
5: 2	I sleep, but my heart is awake; *It is* the voice of my…**beloved [6. dod]**! He knocks, *saying*, "Open for me, my sister, my…**love [17. ra'yah]**, My dove, my perfect one; For my head is covered with dew, My locks with the drops of the night."
5: 4	My **beloved [6. dod]**…put his hand By the latch *of the door,* And my heart yearned for him.
5: 5	I arose to open for my…**beloved [6. dod]**, And my hands dripped *with* myrrh, My fingers with liquid myrrh, On the handles of the lock.
5: 6	I opened for my…**beloved [6. dod]**, But my beloved had turned away *and* was gone. My heart leaped up when he spoke. I sought him, but I could not find him; I called him, but he gave me no answer.
5: 8	I charge you, O daughters of Jerusalem, If you find my…**beloved [6. dod]**, That you tell him I *am*…**lovesick [4. 'ahabah]**!
5: 9	What *is* your…**beloved [6. dod]** More than *another*…**beloved [6. dod]**, O fairest among women? What *is* your…**beloved [6. dod]** More than *another*…**beloved [6. dod]**, That you so charge us?
5:10	My **beloved [6. dod]**…*is* white and ruddy, Chief among ten thousand.
5:16	His mouth *is* most sweet, Yes, he *is* altogether…**lovely [12. mahmad]**. This *is* my **beloved [6. dod]**, And this *is* my friend, O daughters of Jerusalem!

Song of Solomon OLD TESTAMENT VERSE CONCORDANCE

6: 1	Where has your **beloved [6. dod]**...gone, O fairest among women? Where has your **beloved [6. dod]**...turned aside, That we may seek him with you?
6: 2	My **beloved [6. dod]**...has gone to his garden, To the beds of spices, To feed *his flock* in the gardens, And to gather lilies.
6: 3	I *am* my...**beloved's [6. dod]**, And my **beloved [6. dod]**...*is* mine. He feeds *his flock* among the lilies.
6: 4	O my...**love [17. ra'yah]**, you *are as* beautiful as Tirzah, **Lovely [14. na'veh]**...as Jerusalem, Awesome as *an army* with banners!
7: 6	How fair and how pleasant you are, O...**love [4. 'ahabah]**, with your delights!
7: 9	And the roof of your mouth like the best wine. *The wine* goes *down* smoothly for my...**beloved [6. dod]**, Moving gently the lips of sleepers.
7:10	I *am* my...**beloved's [6. dod]**, And his desire *is* toward me.
7:11	Come, my...**beloved [6. dod]**, Let us go forth to the field; Let us lodge in the villages.
7:12	Let us get up early to the vineyards; Let us see if the vine has budded, *Whether* the grape blossoms are open, *And* the pomegranates are in bloom. There I will give you my...**love [6. dod]**.
7:13	The mandrakes give off a fragrance, And at our gates *are* pleasant *fruits*, All manner, new and old, Which I have laid up for you, my...**beloved [6. dod]**.
8: 4	I charge you, O daughters of Jerusalem, Do not stir up nor awaken...**love [4. 'ahabah]** Until it pleases.
8: 5	Who *is* this coming up from the wilderness, Leaning upon her...**beloved [6. dod]**? I awakened you under the apple tree. There your mother brought you forth; There she *who* bore you brought *you* forth.

8: 6		Set me as a seal upon your heart, As a seal upon your arm; For **love** [4. 'ahabah]...*is as* strong as death, Jealousy *as* cruel as the grave; Its flames *are* flames of fire, A most vehement flame.
8: 7		Many waters cannot quench...**love** [4. 'ahabah], Nor can the floods drown it. If a man would give for...**love** [4. 'ahabah] All the wealth of his house, It would be utterly despised.
8:14		Make haste, my...**beloved** [6. dod], And be like a gazelle Or a young stag On the mountains of spices.

❏ Isaiah

1:23		Your princes *are* rebellious, And companions of thieves; Everyone **loves** [3. 'ahab]...bribes, And follows after rewards. They do not defend the fatherless, Nor does the cause of the widow come before them.
5: 1		Now let me sing to my...**Well-beloved** [22. yadid] A song of my **Beloved** [6. dod]...regarding His vineyard: My **Well-beloved** [22. yadid]...has a vineyard On a very fruitful hill.
38:17		Indeed *it was* for *my own* peace *That* I had great bitterness; But You have **lovingly** *delivered* [10. hashaq]...my soul from the pit of corruption, For You have cast all my sins behind Your back.
40: 6		The voice said, "Cry out!" And he said, "What shall I cry?" "All flesh *is* grass, And all its **loveliness** [11. hesed]...*is* like the flower of the field."
43: 4		"Since you were precious in My sight, You have been honored, And I have **loved** [3. 'ahab]...you; Therefore I will give men for you, And people for your life."

48:14	"All of you, assemble yourselves, and hear! Who among them has declared these *things*? The LORD **loves** [3. **'ahab**]...him; He shall do His pleasure on Babylon, And His arm *shall be against* the Chaldeans."
56: 6	"Also the sons of the foreigner Who join themselves to the LORD, to serve Him, And to **love** [3. **'ahab**]...the name of the LORD, to be His servants— Everyone who keeps from defiling the Sabbath, And holds fast My covenant—"
56:10	His watchmen *are* blind, They are all ignorant; They *are* all dumb dogs, They cannot bark; Sleeping, lying down, **loving** [3. **'ahab**]...to slumber.
57: 8	"Also behind the doors and their posts You have set up your remembrance; For you have uncovered yourself *to those other* than Me, And have gone up to them; You have enlarged your bed And made *a covenant* with them; You have **loved**[3. **'ahab**]...their bed, Where you saw *their* nudity."
61: 8	"For I, the LORD, **love** [3. **'ahab**]...justice; I hate robbery for burnt offering; I will direct their work in truth, And will make with them an everlasting covenant."
63: 7	I will mention the **lovingkindnesses** [11. **hesed**]...of the LORD *And* the praises of the LORD, According to all that the LORD has bestowed on us, And the great goodness toward the house of Israel, Which He has bestowed on them according to His mercies, According to the multitude of His...**lovingkindnesses** [11. **hesed**].
63: 9	In all their affliction He was afflicted, And the Angel of His Presence saved them; In His **love** [4. **'ahabah**]...and in His pity He redeemed them; And He bore them and carried them All the days of old.
66:10	"Rejoice with Jerusalem, And be glad with her, all you who **love** [3. **'ahab**]...her; Rejoice for joy with her, all you who mourn for her;"

❏ Jeremiah

2: 2   "Go and cry in the hearing of Jerusalem, saying, 'Thus says the LORD:

> "I remember you,
> The kindness of your youth,
> The **love** [4. 'ahabah]...of your betrothal,
> When you went after Me in the wilderness,
> In a land not sown." ' "

2:25   "Withhold your foot from being unshod, and your throat from thirst.
But you said, 'There is no hope.
No! For I have **loved** [3. 'ahab]...aliens, and after them I will go.' "

2:33   "Why do you beautify your way to seek...**love** [4. 'ahabah]?
Therefore you have also taught
The wicked women your ways."

3: 1   "They say, 'If a man divorces his wife,
And she goes from him
And becomes another man's,
May he return to her again?'
Would not that land be greatly polluted?
But you have played the harlot with many...**lovers** [18. rea'];
Yet return to Me," says the LORD.

4:30   "And *when* you *are* plundered,
What will you do?
Though you clothe yourself with crimson,
Though you adorn *yourself* with ornaments of gold,
Though you enlarge your eyes with paint,
In vain you will make yourself fair;
Your **lovers** [1. 'agab]...will despise you;
They will seek your life."

5:31   "The prophets prophesy falsely,
And the priests rule by their *own* power;
And My people **love** [3. 'ahab]...*to have it* so.
But what will you do in the end?"

6: 2   "I have likened the daughter of Zion
To a **lovely** [14. na'veh]...and delicate woman."

8: 2   "They shall spread them before the sun and the moon and all the host of heaven, which they have **loved** [3. 'ahab]...and which they have served and after which they have walked, which they have sought and which they have worshiped. They shall not be gathered nor buried; they shall be like refuse on the face of the earth."

9:24	"But let him who glories glory in this, That he understands and knows Me, That I *am* the LORD, exercising...**lovingkindness** [11. hesed], judgment, and righteousness in the earth. For in these I delight," says the LORD.
11:15	"What has My **beloved** [22. yadid]...to do in My house, Having done lewd deeds with many? And the holy flesh has passed from you. When you do evil, then you rejoice."
11:16	The LORD called your name, Green Olive Tree, **Lovely** [23. yapheh]...*and* of Good Fruit. With the noise of a great tumult He has kindled fire on it, And its branches are broken.
12: 7	"I have forsaken My house, I have left My heritage; I have given the **dearly beloved** [24. yedidut]...of My soul into the hand of her enemies."
14:10	Thus says the LORD to this people: "Thus they have **loved** [3. 'ahab]...to wander; They have not restrained their feet. Therefore the LORD does not accept them; He will remember their iniquity now, And punish their sins."
16: 5	For thus says the LORD: "Do not enter the house of mourning, nor go to lament or bemoan them; for I have taken away My peace from this people," says the LORD, "**lovingkindness** [11. hesed]...and mercies."
22:20	"Go up to Lebanon, and cry out, And lift up your voice in Bashan; Cry from Abarim, For all your **lovers** [3. 'ahab]...are destroyed."
22:22	"The wind shall eat up all your rulers, And your **lovers** [3. 'ahab]...shall go into captivity; Surely then you will be ashamed and humiliated For all your wickedness."
30:14	"All your **lovers** [3. 'ahab]...have forgotten you; They do not seek you; For I have wounded you with the wound of an enemy, With the chastisement of a cruel one, For the multitude of your iniquities, *Because* your sins have increased."

31: 3   The LORD has appeared of old to me, *saying:*
"Yes, I have **loved** [3. 'ahab]...you with an everlasting...**love**
    [4. 'ahabah];
Therefore with **lovingkindness** [11. hesed]...I have drawn you."

32:18   "You show **lovingkindness** [11. hesed]...to thousands, and repay the iniquity of the fathers into the bosom of their children after them—the Great, the Mighty God, whose name *is* the LORD of hosts."

❏ Lamentations

1: 2   She weeps bitterly in the night,
Her tears *are* on her cheeks;
Among all her...**lovers** [3. 'ahab]
She has none to comfort *her*.
All her friends have dealt treacherously with her;
They have become her enemies.

1:19   "I called for my...**lovers** [3. 'ahab],
But they deceived me;
My priests and my elders
Breathed their last in the city,
While they sought food
To restore their life."

❏ Ezekiel

16: 8   "When I passed by you again and looked upon you, indeed your time *was* the time of...**love** [6. dod]; so I spread My wing over you and covered your nakedness. Yes, I swore an oath to you and entered into a covenant with you, and you became Mine," says the Lord GOD.

16:33   "Men make payment to all harlots, but you made your payments to all your...**lovers** [3. 'ahab], and hired them to come to you from all around for your harlotry."

16:36   'Thus says the Lord GOD: "Because your filthiness was poured out and your nakedness uncovered in your harlotry with your...**lovers** [3. 'ahab], and with all your abominable idols, and because of the blood of your children which you gave to them," '

16:37   "surely, therefore, I will gather all your **lovers** [3. 'ahab]...with whom you took pleasure, all those you...**loved** [3. 'ahab], *and* all those you hated; I will gather them from all around against you and will uncover your nakedness to them, that they may see all your nakedness."

16:41	"They shall burn your houses with fire, and execute judgments on you in the sight of many women; and I will make you cease playing the harlot, and you shall no longer hire...**lovers** [6. dod]."
23: 5	"Oholah played the harlot even though she was Mine; And she lusted for her...**lovers** [3. 'ahab], the neighboring Assyrians,"
23: 9	"Therefore I have delivered her Into the hand of her...**lovers** [3. 'ahab], Into the hand of the Assyrians, For whom she lusted."
23:17	"Then the Babylonians came to her, into the bed of...**love** [6. dod], And they defiled her with their immorality; So she was defiled by them, and alienated herself from them."
23:22	"Therefore, Oholibah, thus says the Lord GOD: 'Behold, I will stir up your **lovers** [3. 'ahab]...against you, From whom you have alienated yourself, And I will bring them against you from every side:' "
33:31	"So they come to you as people do, they sit before you *as* My people, and they hear your words, but they do not do them; for with their mouth they show...**much love** [2. 'agabim]...*but* their hearts pursue their *own* gain."
33:32	"Indeed you *are* to them as a **very lovely** [2. 'agabim]...song of one who has a pleasant voice and can play well on an instrument; for they hear your words, but they do not do them."

❏ Daniel

4:12	"Its leaves *were*...**lovely** [20. shappir], Its fruit abundant, And in it *was* food for all. The beasts of the field found shade under it, The birds of the heavens dwelt in its branches, And all flesh was fed from it."
4:21	"whose leaves *were* **lovely** [20. shappir]...and its fruit abundant, in which *was* food for all, under which the beasts of the field dwelt, and in whose branches the birds of the heaven had their home—"
9: 4	And I prayed to the LORD my God, and made confession, and said, "O Lord, great and awesome God, who keeps His covenant and mercy with those who **love** [3. 'ahab]...Him, and with those who keep His commandments,"

9:23	"At the beginning of your supplications the command went out, and I have come to tell *you,* for you *are*...**greatly beloved** [9. hamudot]; therefore consider the matter, and understand the vision:"
10:11	And he said to me, "O Daniel, man...**greatly beloved** [9. hamudot], understand the words that I speak to you, and stand upright, for I have now been sent to you." While he was speaking this word to me, I stood trembling.
10:19	And he said, "O man...**greatly beloved** [9. hamudot], fear not! Peace *be* to you; be strong, yes, be strong!" So when he spoke to me I was strengthened, and said, "Let my lord speak, for you have strengthened me."

❏ Hosea

2: 5	"For their mother has played the harlot; She who conceived them has behaved shamefully. For she said, 'I will go after my...**lovers** [3. 'ahab], Who give *me* my bread and my water, My wool and my linen, My oil and my drink.' "
2: 7	"She will chase her...**lovers** [3. 'ahab], But not overtake them; Yes, she will seek them, but not find *them.* Then she will say, 'I will go and return to my first husband, For then *it was* better for me than now.' "
2:10	"Now I will uncover her lewdness in the sight of her...**lovers** [3. 'ahab], And no one shall deliver her from My hand."
2:12	"And I will destroy her vines and her fig trees, Of which she has said, 'These *are* my wages that my **lovers** [3. 'ahab]...have given me.' So I will make them a forest, And the beasts of the field shall eat them."
2:13	"I will punish her For the days of the Baals to which she burned incense. She decked herself with her earrings and jewelry, And went after her...**lovers** [3. 'ahab], But Me she forgot," says the LORD.
2:19	"I will betroth you to Me forever; Yes, I will betroth you to Me In righteousness and justice, In **lovingkindness** [11. hesed]...and mercy;"

3: 1	Then the LORD said to me, "Go again, **love** [3. **'ahab**]...a woman *who is* **loved** [3. **'ahab**]...by a **lover** [18. **rea'**]...and is committing adultery, just like the **love** [4. **'ahabah**]...of the LORD for the children of Israel, who look to other gods and **love** [3. **'ahab**]...*the* raisin cakes *of the pagans.*"
4:18	"Their drink is rebellion, They commit harlotry continually. Her rulers **dearly love** [3. **'ahab**]...dishonor."
8: 9	"For they have gone up to Assyria, *Like* a wild donkey alone by itself; Ephraim has hired...**lovers** [3. **'ahab**]."
9: 1	Do not rejoice, O Israel, with joy like *other* peoples, For you have played the harlot against your God. You have **made love** [3. **'ahab**]...*for* hire on every threshing floor.
9:10	"I found Israel Like grapes in the wilderness; I saw your fathers As the firstfruits on the fig tree in its first season. *But* they went to Baal Peor, And separated themselves *to that* shame; They became an abomination like the thing they...**loved** [3. **'ahab**]."
9:15	"All their wickedness *is* in Gilgal, For there I hated them. Because of the evil of their deeds I will drive them from My house; I will **love** [4. **'ahabah**]...them no more. All their princes *are* rebellious."
10:11	"Ephraim *is* a trained heifer That **loves** [3. **'ahab**]...to thresh *grain;* But I harnessed her fair neck, I will make Ephraim pull *a plow.* Judah shall plow; Jacob shall break his clods."
11: 1	"When Israel *was* a child, I **loved** [3. **'ahab**]...him, And out of Egypt I called My son."
11: 4	"I drew them with gentle cords, With bands of...**love** [4. **'ahabah**], And I was to them as those who take the yoke from their neck. I stooped *and* fed them."

12:7 "A cunning Canaanite!
Deceitful scales *are* in his hand;
He **loves** [3. 'ahab]...to oppress."

14:4 "I will heal their backsliding,
I will **love** [3. 'ahab]...them freely,
For My anger has turned away from him."

❏ Amos

4: 5 "Offer a sacrifice of thanksgiving with leaven,
Proclaim *and* announce the freewill offerings;
For this you...**love** [3. 'ahab],
You children of Israel!"
Says the Lord GOD.

5:15 Hate evil, **love** [3. 'ahab]...good;
Establish justice in the gate.
It may be that the LORD God of hosts
Will be gracious to the remnant of Joseph.

❏ Jonah

4: 2 So he prayed to the LORD, and said, "Ah, LORD, was not this what I said when I was still in my country? Therefore I fled previously to Tarshish; for I know that You *are* a gracious and merciful God, slow to anger and abundant in...**lovingkindness** [11. hesed], One who relents from doing harm."

❏ Micah

3: 2 "You who hate good and **love** [3. 'ahab]...evil;
Who strip the skin from My people,
And the flesh from their bones;"

6: 8 He has shown you, O man, what *is* good;
And what does the LORD require of you
But to do justly,
To **love** [4. 'ahabah]...mercy,
And to walk humbly with your God?

❏ Zephaniah

3:17 "The LORD your God in your midst,
The Mighty One, will save;
He will rejoice over you with gladness,

He will quiet *you* with His...love [4. 'ahabah],
He will rejoice over you with singing."

❏ Zechariah

8:17 " 'Let none of you think evil in your heart against your neighbor;
And do not love [3. 'ahab]...a false oath.
For all these *are things* that I hate,'
Says the LORD."

8:19 "Thus says the LORD of hosts:

'The fast of the fourth *month*,
The fast of the fifth,
The fast of the seventh,
And the fast of the tenth,
Shall be joy and gladness and cheerful feasts
For the house of Judah.
Therefore love [3. 'ahab]...truth and peace.' "

❏ Malachi

1: 2 "I have loved [3. 'ahab]...you," says the LORD.
"Yet you say, 'In what way have You loved [3. 'ahab]...us?'
Was not Esau Jacob's brother?"
Says the LORD.
"Yet Jacob I have...loved [3. 'ahab];"

2:11 Judah has dealt treacherously,
And an abomination has been committed in Israel and in
  Jerusalem,
For Judah has profaned
The Lord's holy *institution* which He...loves [3. 'ahab]:
He has married the daughter of a foreign god.

Prayer

Father God, You are love, and You live in the hearts of your born-again people. May our relationship with You be free and open and satisfying. May we yield to the wisdom of Your Holy Spirit at all times. Bless us in our relationships with others, with family members, brothers and sisters in Christ, and those with whom we work. May we radiate Your love like the sun, regardless of the response we get. In Jesus' name. Amen.

Self-Study Assignments

Here are some self-study questions and exercises:

1. Did you accept Jesus as your Savior for the first time or rededicate your life to Him as you read this book? If so, I would be honored if you would let me know at: PastorMike@michaelchristian.us.

2. Have you formed the daily habit of meditating in God's Word at a set time?

3. Have you copied the *You and God* Scriptures in your own handwriting? Have you tried it? Is something holding you back? They are listed to help you meditate in God's Word though the powerful meditation technique known as Scripture handwriting.

4. Name three beneficial things that happened while hand copying Scriptures?

5. Identify your seven favorite love Scriptures from the Old and New Testaments.

   _____
   _____
   _____
   _____
   _____
   _____
   _____

6. Which characteristics of love from the Love Chapter are you already practicing? Which are difficult for you? Does it help to work on the top two, patience and kindness?

7. How would you define the differences between *agape, philia,* and *eros?*

8. Are you focusing on living Christ's New Commandment? What does it mean to love as Christ has loved you?

9. Which New and Old Testament word definitions did you find the most interesting?

10. What is the most important thing you've learned from your study of love? How is it affecting your everyday behavior?

Bibliography

Abbott-Smith, G. *A Manual Greek Lexicon of the New Testament*. Edinburgh: T. & T. Clark, 1948.

Barclay, William. *More New Testament Words*. New York: Harper & Brothers, 1958

Bauer, Walter, William F. Arndt, F. Wilbur Gingrich, Frederick W., Danker. *A Greek-English Lexicon of the New Testament and Other Early Christian Literature*. Chicago: The University of Chicago Press, 1979.

Brenton, Sir Lancelot C. L. *The Septuagint with Apocrypha: Greek and English*. Peabody, MA: Hendrickson, 1987.

Brown, Francis, S. R. Driver, Charles A. Briggs. *The New Brown-Driver-Briggs-Gesenius Hebrew and English Lexicon*. Peabody, MA: Hendrickson, 1979.

Brown, Francis, Samuel Rolles Driver, and Charles Augustus Briggs. *Enhanced Brown-Driver-Briggs Hebrew and English Lexicon*. Oxford: Clarendon Press, 1977.

Enns, Gaylord. *Love Revolution*. Chico, CA: Love Revolution Press, 2022.

Gesenius, William. *Gesenius' Hebrew and Chaldee Lexicon to the Old Testament Scriptures*. Translated by Samuel Prideaux Tregelles. Grand Rapids, MI: Baker, 1979.

Harris, R. Laird, Gleason L. Archer, Jr., Bruce K. Waltke, eds. *Theological Wordbook of the Old Testament*. Chicago: Moody Press, 1980.

Hatch, Erwin, Henry A. Redpath. *A Concordance to the Septuagint*, 2 Vols. Grand Rapids, MI: Baker, 1987.

Kittel, Gerhard, Gerhard Friedrich, and Geoffrey William Bromiley, eds. *Theological Dictionary of the New Testament*, 10 Vols. Grand Rapids, MI: Eerdmans, 1985.

Kohlenberger, John R. *The NIV Interlinear Hebrew-English Old Testament*. Grand Rapids, MI: Zondervan, 1987.

Logos Bible Software. https://www.logos.com/.

Louw, Johannes P., Eugene Albert Nida. *Greek-English Lexicon of the New Testament: Based on Semantic Domains*. New York: United Bible Societies, 1996.

Moulton, James Hope, George Milligan. *The Vocabulary of the Greek Testament*. Grand Rapids, MI: Eerdmans, 1985.

Robertson, A.T. *Word Pictures in the New Testament*. Nashville, TN: Broadman Press, 1933.

Scherman, Rabbi Nosson, Rabbi Meir Zlotowitz, Gen. Eds. *The Chumash, The Stone Edition*. Brooklyn, NY: Mesorah Publications, Ltd., 2012.

Spicq, Ceslas, and James D. Ernest. *Theological Lexicon of the New Testament*. Peabody, MA: Hendrickson, 1994.

Strong, James. *Enhanced Strong's Lexicon*. Woodside Bible Fellowship, 1995.

Strong, James. *The Exhaustive Concordance of the Bible*. Nashville, TN: Abingdon Press, 1973.

Swanson, James. *Dictionary of Biblical Languages with Semantic Domains: Greek (New Testament)*. Oak Harbor, WA: Logos Research Systems, Inc., 1997.

Thayer, Joseph Henry. *The New Thayer's Greek-English Lexicon of the New Testament*. Peabody, MA: Hendrickson, 1981.

The Lexham Analytical Lexicon to the Greek New Testament. Logos Bible Software, 2011.

The Zondervan Parallel New Testament in Greek and English. Grand Rapids, MI: Zondervan, 1975.

Thomas, Robert L. *New American Standard Hebrew-Aramaic and Greek Dictionaries : Updated Edition*. Anaheim: Foundation Publications, Inc., 1998.

Trench, Richard C. *Synonyms of The New Testament*. Digitized by Ted Hildebrandt, Gordon College, Wenham, MA, 2006.

Vincent, Marvin Richardson. *Word Studies in the New Testament*. New York: Charles Scribner's Sons, 1887.

Vine, W. E., Merrill F. Unger, and William White, Jr. *Vine's Complete Expository Dictionary of Old and New Testament Words*. Nashville, TN: Thomas Nelson, 1996.

Wilson, William. *Wilson's Old Testament Word Studies*. McLean, VA: MacDonald Publishing Co.

Young, Robert. *Analytical Concordance to the Bible*. Grand Rapids, MI: Eerdmans, 1973.

Let all that you do be done with love.

—1 Corinthians 16:14

The grace of the Lord Jesus Christ, and the love of God,
and the communion of the Holy Spirit be with you all.
Amen.

—2 Corinthians 13:14

www.ingramcontent.com/pod-product-compliance
Lightning Source LLC
Chambersburg PA
CBHW080346300426
44110CB00019B/2523